OF ANGER AND FRUSTRATION

PAM *and* JOHN VREDEVELT

Multnomah® Publishers *Sisters, Oregon*

LETTING GO OF ANGER AND FRUSTRATION
published by Multnomah Publishers, Inc.

International Standard Book Number: 1-57673-926-0

Cover design by The Office of Bill Chiaravalle
Cover image by Artville

Printed in the United States of America

For information:
MULTNOMAH PUBLISHERS, INC. • P.O. 1720 • SISTERS, OR 97759

Vredevelt, Pam W., 1955–
Letting go of anger and frustration / by Pam Vredevelt and John Vredevelt.
p. cm.
ISBN 1-57673-926-0 (pbk.)
1. Anger—Religious aspects—Christianity. 2. Frustration—Religious aspects—Christianity. I. Vredevelt, John, 1955– II. Title.
BV4627.A5 V74 2002
152.4'7—dc21

2002003689

02 03 04 05 06 07 08—10 9 8 7 6 5 4 3 2 1 0

Dedication

To the courageous individuals who allow us the
privilege of supporting them
as they do the hard work of letting go.

ACKNOWLEDGMENTS

WE WANT TO SAY A HEARTFELT THANKS TO DON AND BRENDA Jacobson, Bill Jensen, and the entire family at Multnomah. We appreciate your help in fulfilling our dream of coauthoring together.

Our special thanks to Judith St. Pierre for sticking with us through the Letting Go series, and for your tremendous editorial gifts. Your polishing touches create luster.

And finally we want to thank our children, our dear friends and family, and East Hill Church for their prayers, support, and encouragement. You keep us going and we love you.

Pam and John Vredevelt

Introduction

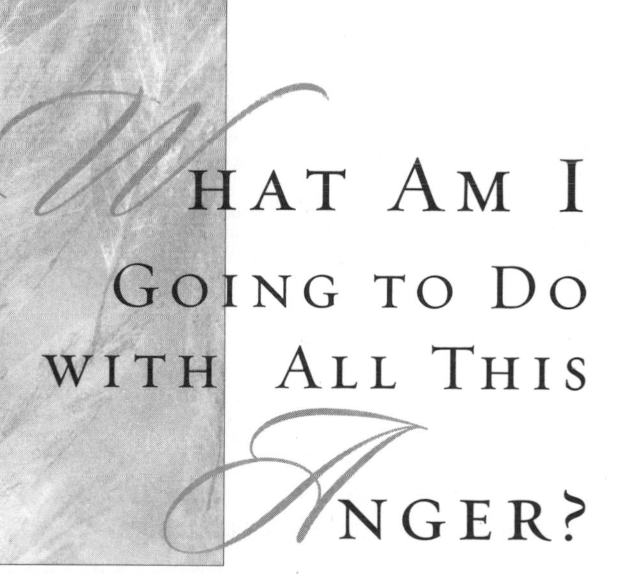

What Am I Going to Do with All This Anger?

ON SEPTEMBER 11, 2001, TERRORISTS HIJACKED FOUR commercial jetliners and turned them into weapons of mass murder. They crashed two of the planes into the World Trade Center and one into the Pentagon. The fourth, most likely destined for the White House or the U.S. Capitol, crashed into a field in Pennsylvania thanks to the heroic and self-sacrificing efforts of some of the passengers and crew.

For days on end we saw the televised images of the attack on the World Trade Center repeated nonstop:

Jetliners slamming into the twin towers.

Flames roaring toward the sky, smoke billowing over New York City.

People, some of them on fire, leaping out of windows.

Crowds covered with ash, running through the debris in lower Manhattan.

The horrific impact of this attack was immediate and profound. In the aftermath, New York had a hole in its skyline, and America had a hole in its heart. National landmarks fell, and our frustration rose as we became keenly aware of our powerlessness to prevent such terrible tragedies. When we dug in the rubble of our souls, we found what President Bush identified in his national address as an "unyielding anger."

This unyielding anger was driven deeper into our psyches as we watched the news coverage of Palestinians celebrating in the streets—men, women, and children cheering our devastation, praising Allah for the victory, and burning American flags in public squares. These images only fueled our anger, and suspicion began to taint our views of everyone from "that part of the world." As frustration and anger simmered in my own soul, I saw myself making them a target of my anger. And I didn't like what I saw.

A week after the terrorist attacks, my husband, John, and I boarded a plane in San Francisco to fly to Hawaii to celebrate our twenty-fifth wedding anniversary. We had flown this leg many times to visit friends in Kauai, and the passengers, enjoying the start of a lovely vacation, were usually in a jovial mood. But this flight was different. A heavy cloud of grief permeated the atmosphere as somber passengers quietly took their seats. There was a noticeable strain of anxiety under the polite smiles of the flight attendants.

John and I were on guard. We watched the people boarding the plane and took extra care to observe those sitting around us. I noticed that John looked toward the back of the plane a few times, and I figured he had seen someone he knew. He hadn't. He was looking at a man sitting three rows behind us on the aisle—a man who looked as though he may have been from the Middle East. The last time John turned around, a large man sitting across the aisle behind us made eye contact with him, nodded his head, and winked, sending an obvious signal: *I see that guy, too. If he tries anything, you and I will take him out.*

I was grateful that they were on alert but troubled by my own raw prejudice against someone of a different ethnic background. All the poor guy did was "look the part," and I rendered him guilty. I knew that these feelings were the result of the dreadful events of September 11, but even so, I didn't like them.

John and I weren't the only ones wrestling with these internal conflicts. As media coverage of the events continued, it became evident that anti-Arab, anti-Muslim sentiment was on the rise in America. As a result of the deep-seated anger the nation was experiencing, people screamed, "Close the borders! Stop immigration! Send the Arabs home!" Worse, some people committed hate crimes.

The anger is real. Given the situation, it is natural. And it is legitimate. Americans were and still are morally outraged.

Though I don't like to admit it, it really doesn't take something big like a terrorist attack to evoke feelings of anger and frustration. Simple little things can do it: realizing we are in the slowest-moving line at the grocery when we're running late for our next appointment, losing our car keys, seeing a maniac driver wave "international" hand signals at us as he passes us going ninety miles an hour, having our computer malfunction and shut down halfway into a chapter. Like I said, it doesn't take much to light the fuse.

Whatever the reason for our anger, when it surfaces, we need to ask ourselves some important questions:

What am I going to do with all this anger?

How can I process it in healthy ways?

Is it possible to remain passionate about right and wrong without becoming poisoned by bitterness and hate?

Can I somehow open my clenched fists and let the anger go?

Perhaps some of you are thinking, *I don't want to let it go!* Indeed, there is something very satisfying about hanging on to anger. It's empowering. An adrenaline surge coupled with a quest for justice is energizing. But unfortunately, taking out our anger on others usually makes things worse. At first it might feel good to lash out, but as soon as we do, we may start to feel guilty for our impulsive, irrational acts, which are contrary to how we truly want to behave. Or, as a feedback loop occurs, we may find ourselves even angrier than we initially were.

So what's the answer? Is anger something bad that we should avoid? Is it something good that we should encourage? Can we truly love God and be angry at the same time? Can we express anger without harming others or ourselves? We must find answers to these questions, lest we harbor our anger and become like the vicious terrorists we condemn. Make no mistake: Anger begets anger. Those who allow themselves to become steeped in rage destroy themselves as well as others. September 11, 2001, is a gruesome illustration of murderous rage taken to the extreme.

I'm not sure what prompted you to pick up this book. Perhaps you're confused by your own feelings of anger. Perhaps others have encouraged you to find help with handling this troublesome emotion. Maybe you typically stuff your anger, which leaves you feeling tired and depressed. Or maybe you feel like a walking time bomb on the verge of exploding. Whatever the case may be, it is our hope that the timeless truths in this book will lead you to new levels of emotional and spiritual health by helping you understand your anger and process it constructively.

This is the third book in the Letting Go series. I wrote the first two books, *Letting Go of Disappointments and Painful Losses* and *Letting Go of Worry and Anxiety,* by myself, with the skillful assistance of the staff at Multnomah Publishers. I am writing this book with my husband, an assistant pastor at East Hill Church in Gresham, Oregon. John has been on the church staff since 1976 and has many years of experience as a counselor and educator specializing in anger management.

In the pages that follow, you will read stories about our personal struggles with managing anger. You'll see that anger has many faces. While John and I have many similar interests, we are very different from each other, and some of our greatest battles have occurred as the result of the different ways we handle our frustrations. But one thing is certain: As we have worked through our problems with anger and learned to appreciate our differences, we have become healing agents in each other's lives.

Both of us, however, are quick to admit that we haven't "arrived." Even after twenty-five years of conscientiously working on managing our anger wisely, something inevitably happens to remind us that we need God's help to be who we want to be. We are definitely in process.

We want to share portions of that process with you and give you some tools to manage your anger. It is our sincere hope that you will glean useful insights from the Bible, from our research and clinical experience, and from our successes and mistakes. We pray that God will help you understand what makes you angry and how you are likely to react, and then help you use the tools offered here to constructively process your anger and eventually...let it go.

Holding on to anger is like holding

on to a hot coal.

We are the ones who end up getting burned.

Chapter One

Remember: It's Okay to Be Angry

Go ahead and be angry. You do well to be angry—

but don't use your anger as fuel for revenge.

EPHESIANS 4:26, *THE MESSAGE*

FOR MANY YEARS NOW, JOHN HAS TAUGHT ANGER management classes. Some of those who attend his courses are there only because the court has required them to seek professional help. Others are average, get-up-and-go-to-work kinds of men and women who now and then lash out at their coworkers, spouses, or kids. Whatever their background, they all have one pressing need: to learn to manage their anger constructively. John's goal is to give them the tools they need to do that.

John's students are not alone in their need to learn how to break destructive anger patterns. Research conducted during the 1990s showed that domestic violence was the number one reason women visited hospital emergency rooms. Focus on the Family, Dr. James Dobson's organization, surveyed children across America from all economic strata, asking them this question: If you could change one thing about your parents, what would it be? Ninety-six percent of the children said, "I wish they wouldn't get mad at me so much." Parents obviously struggle with anger. In fact, there isn't a person alive who doesn't find it difficult to handle anger now and then. And when anger is mismanaged, it can carry a very high cost.

One of the first things John does at the beginning of a class is to ask each person to complete this sentence: "I get angry when…" Over the years, the answers have been remarkably similar. Do any of these responses hit a nerve in you? If so, welcome to the human race. If not, please see your doctor to determine whether you have a pulse!

I get angry when...

- I'm late and can't find my car keys.
- I make stupid mistakes.
- I know that someone isn't listening to me.
- I ask my kids to do something and they argue with me.
- I think someone is talking down to me.
- I feel controlled.
- I can't control things or make things work out.
- I'm the target of inconsiderate drivers.
- I feel threatened.
- I'm treated unfairly.
- I'm betrayed.
- I hear someone calling another person derogatory names.
- I feel that God doesn't answer my prayers.
- I see innocent people suffer.

Our responses to situations like these will differ depending on how much importance we attach to them. We aren't likely to get frustrated or angry about something that isn't important to us. The more it matters, the more intense our emotional response. Anger can be viewed as part of a continuum:

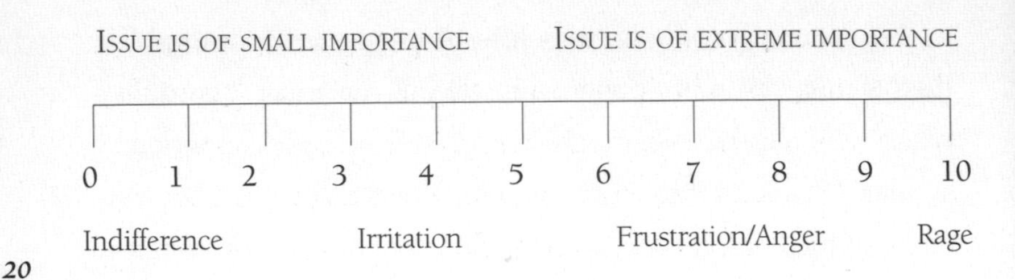

I'm sure that, with the exception of terrorists and their sympathizers, there were very few people who weren't angry in the aftermath of the terrorist attacks of September 11, 2001. In fact, in the face of this and other evil acts, the absence of anger may indicate apathy, indifference, or a lack of compassion for others.

Anger is a legitimate response to certain situations. It is not a bad emotion.

In his classes, John makes it clear that anger is a legitimate response to certain situations. "Our goal," he says, "is *not* to teach you how to stop being angry. We're starting this course with the assumption that anger is not a bad emotion. It's a normal, healthy emotion, and it's important that we acknowledge and feel it. And while it's a healthy emotion, it can also be a challenging one, as most of you already know.

"I'll say it again: The goal of this class isn't to help you stop feeling anger. When we try to deny or repress our feelings, we misspend our energies. Feelings that are stuffed don't go away; they just remain hidden. And when they remain hidden, they gain control over us. I've met some people who have hidden their feelings for so long that when they try to access them, they can't. They may not feel much anger, but they have no joy either.

"It's okay to be angry. But have you ever noticed how the word *anger* is one letter short of *danger*? The way we process and express our anger can be good or it can be bad. The goal of this class is to help us learn how to be angry without blowing it. If we don't process our anger properly, we can create danger for ourselves and for others."

Anger is part of God's original design. In the Bible there are 150 references to God's anger, and because He created us in His image, we too have the capacity to be angry. Does this mean that God is an irritable tyrant? The only way we can answer that question is to examine the life of Jesus Christ, who fully revealed God's nature. There we see that God's anger is the result of His justice and His love and compassion for mankind.

Anger is part of God's original design.

Time and again in the Bible we read that Jesus was "moved with compassion." The Greek word for *compassion* literally means to experience a gut-wrenching sensation. His heart broke when He saw people who were in desperate need, unfairly oppressed, or grossly mistreated. A strong sense of empathy led Him to feed the hungry, heal the sick, comfort the mourning, and raise the dead. He grieved over the injustices He witnessed…and they made Him angry.

In Mark 3:5 we find the Pharisees condemning Jesus for healing a man on the Sabbath. According to their teaching, no work was allowed on the Sabbath, and they considered healing a form of work. The Scripture says that Jesus was "grieved for the hardness of their hearts" and that He "looked round about on them with anger" (KJV).

Mark 10:13–16 tells us that Jesus became angry with His disciples when they tried to stop a group of children from approaching Him. He sternly rebuked them, told them to let the children come to Him, and then laid His hands on the little ones and blessed them.

Perhaps the best-known example of Jesus' anger is found in Mark 11:15–17. Merchants and moneylenders had set up their businesses in the temple courts. Incensed, Jesus overturned their tables. "Is it not written, My house shall be called of all nations the house of prayer?" He cried. "But ye have made it a den of thieves" (v. 17, KJV).

Jesus was not indifferent to the sin and suffering in this world. In fact, it made Him angry, and His anger drove Him to take action on behalf of others, including laying down His own life so that the rest of us could be forgiven of our sins and thus receive eternal life. Jesus got angry, but He used His anger as God intended—for good.

Jesus got angry, but He used His anger as God intended—for good.

Anger, properly channeled and controlled, is a good thing—a God-given thing. Sometimes our anger is an indication that we have a strong sense of justice, and people who become angry about injustice often make our world a better place to live. Martin Luther's anger about the religious abuses of his time ushered in the Reformation. The Thirteenth Amendment was the fruit of agitation by abolitionists who were angry about the enslavement of human beings. Suffragettes angry about their inability to vote initiated a campaign that resulted in the passage of the Nineteenth Amendment. Martin Luther King's anger about racism led to the Civil Rights Act of 1964. All these people were angry, but they channeled their anger into positive action that brought about social reform. Certainly our national anger about terrorist attacks is a positive force that energizes the mission to bring to justice those responsible.

We all get angry, and it's okay to be angry.

Like a chainsaw, anger is not inherently destructive. It's a God-given emotion that has a function. But it can be helpful or harmful, depending on how we use it. If we don't learn how to process and express it in healthy ways, the results can be ruinous. To avoid these disasters and turn our anger toward good ends, we need to know what causes it and how we are likely to react when we feel angry. That's the subject of the next chapter.

God has given us permission to be angry.

Chapter Two

Recognize Your Anger Style

Everyone should be quick to listen, slow to speak and slow to become angry, for man's anger does not bring about the righteous life that God desires.

JAMES 1:19–20

MOST OF US KNOW WHAT ANGER FEELS LIKE, BUT DO WE know what it is? *Webster's New World Dictionary* defines it as "a hostile feeling of displeasure because of injury or opposition." Our response to this hostile feeling of displeasure has both biological and learned components.

Biologically, anger is a survival reflex that we use instinctively when we're faced with some sort of threat. We know from medical research that when certain parts of the brain are electrically stimulated, it sends signals to the body to release chemicals into the bloodstream. In turn, these chemicals cause increased heart rate, shallow breathing, tense muscles, flushed skin, increased temperature, perspiration, and even shakiness. Our body goes on alert to protect us from harm and danger.

Anger is a survival reflex that we use instinctively when we're faced with some sort of threat.

Dr. Theo Johnson, who has lectured on anger management for years, uses a clever acronym—RAT—for three basic perceptions that can trigger anger. It stands for Rejection, Attack, or Threat.[1] When we sense one of these, we "smell a rat." We feel anger, and our body prepares for action. Sometimes the energy that anger generates serves to protect us from physical danger. When RATs are around, we instinctively get ready to fight or flee. At other times, anger serves to protect us from psychological danger by preserving our dignity and self-esteem. The human body needs the mechanism of anger. If we didn't have it, we wouldn't be able to protect ourselves—physically or psychologically.

Anger can also be reaction to physical pain. Have you ever stubbed your toe on a piece of furniture and wanted to kick the table that got in your way? Have you ever been physically hurt and instinctively wanted to hurt back? An automatic response like that once left John facing some rather embarrassing consequences. I'll let him tell you the story.

In the fall of 1974, I was a sophomore in college and in the middle of pre-season soccer practice. Our team was preparing for a season of intense competition, and we had high hopes of finishing first in our league. I was determined to give the team my very best.

During the first few weeks of practice, the coach divided the team into two sides and told us to scrimmage against each other. That was my favorite part of practice because it fueled my competitive fire. When the adrenaline kicked in, I focused every ounce of skill and determination to send the ball flying into the goal net.

When I got the ball, I sprinted down the field, dribbling and outmaneuvering the guys who tried to steal it. Making my way to center field, I saw my buddy Ted. That day he was playing on the opposing side, and there he was, running full speed at me. Seconds later we were waging war over the ball with our feet as each of us tried to dominate the other. Before I knew it, he kicked the ball full force into my groin. I reacted instantly by planting my fist on his mouth and knocking him to the ground. One of his teeth sliced my knuckle open, and we both ended up in the emergency room for stitches. I couldn't believe what I had done.

With an inquisitive grin on her face, the nurse cleaning my knuckle glanced over at Ted, who was sitting on a bed across the room. "I noticed that he came in the same time you did," she said. "Am I correct in assuming that your knuckle and his mouth had a head-on collision?"

I was too embarrassed to think that her comment was funny. "Yeah," I replied sheepishly.

She wasn't finished with her interrogation. "What school do you go to?" she asked, raising her eyebrows.

I hesitated. Covering my mouth with my good hand, I whispered, "Multnomah Bible College."

"I'm sorry," she said. "I didn't hear you."

I repeated myself a little louder.

She grinned again, and I expected her next question to be "So, is that how the school teaches you to handle conflict?" But she just said, "Oohhh."

When Ted and I finally made eye contact, I apologized for

overreacting. He forgave me, and we both went back to campus.

The next day, the dean called me into his office. The last time this sort of thing had happened to me was in seventh grade, when I was called into the principal's office after a playground squabble. Since then, I had managed to steer clear of those kinds of situations, but now it was happening again, this time in the worst possible place—Bible college!

With my tail between my legs, I walked into the dean's office and sat down. Even though my actions had been in self-defense, I was still in trouble.

Peering at me, the dean said, "John, I understand that you had a little run-in with one of the other students...and that you belted him in the mouth."

"Yes sir," I said. "That's right."

"John, why did you come to Bible college?" he asked.

I wasn't sure where the conversation was going, but I told him that God had told me to quit my construction job and go to Bible college to prepare for the ministry. I saw a grin tugging at the corner of his mouth, but he quickly regained his composure and, with a very serious expression, said, "So you want to be a minister?"

"Yes sir, I do...if God will still have me," I replied.

"Well, John," he said, "you might want to work on your anger and the way you react to others."

I laughed nervously, told him I agreed with him, and promised it would never happen again.

I made a concerted effort to keep that promise. Ted and I made amends, and neither of us held a grudge. It was a positive ending to a very embarrassing situation.

Anger is an emotion that indicates that something is wrong and needs attention.

RATs can generate anger, and, as in John's case, so can physical pain. Whatever the stimulus, anger is an emotion that indicates that something is wrong and needs attention. Typically we learn to deal with it by observing those around us. During childhood, we watch parents and siblings respond to situations and then mimic their behavior, trying our hand at influencing our environment and learning what works and what doesn't.

One of John's first recollections of an angry outburst was when he was about ten years old:

> I was lying in bed, trying to go to sleep. My older sisters were still up, watching TV in the living room, laughing and talking very loudly. The noise was keeping me awake. I called out several times for them to be quiet, but they ignored me. When I couldn't take it anymore, I got out of bed and yelled at them. After that, they were quiet. I learned that raising my voice got me what I wanted.

John's family outwardly expressed their emotions. They laughed loudly and talked passionately; they were exuberant over joys and emphatic about things that bothered them. As the third of five children, John witnessed the different anger styles of his older and younger siblings. Two of them tended to be compliant peacemakers who hid their anger. The other two were overtly aggressive. His parents also tended to be open with their conflicts and sometimes argued within hearing range of the children. Raised voices were common in his home.

My family modeled other ways of handling anger. As the oldest of three children, I didn't have any older siblings who stirred up conflicts with me. My brother and sister were four and six years behind me, so sibling rivalry really wasn't much of an issue. And I can't remember ever hearing my parents fight. That doesn't mean they didn't have their problems; it just means that we didn't know about them. They kept their conflicts private and tended to handle them quietly. They rarely raised their voices. As a result of this kind of home environment, I tend to hold in my feelings instead of letting them out. If I'm going to err in mismanaging my anger, it's going to be more internal than external. In the early years of our marriage, I had to work very hard at not stuffing my anger.

In our counseling offices, John and I talk to many people who hide their anger because they think they are doing themselves and others a favor. But when we hold our anger in, hoping that it will just go away, we run the risk of creating other problems for ourselves. Stuffing anger doesn't get rid of it. It simply reroutes it. If bottled up, it will find an avenue of escape in our bodies. Psychosomatic disorders such as high blood pressure, headaches, lower-back pain, fatigue, and stomach problems can be the result of repressed anger.

Stuffing anger doesn't get rid of it.

It simply reroutes it.

Holding in our anger can injure our bodies, and it can also damage our relationships by keeping us from working through conflicts and getting beyond them. I recently met with a woman who described such an impasse:

> Jim called me from the airport and asked me to come pick him up. He had caught an earlier flight, which landed three hours ahead of his planned schedule. I was just walking out the door, as I had to drop off our son at basketball practice on my way to his parent-teacher conference. When I told Jim what I was in the process of doing, he said, "I'll catch a cab," and then hung up the phone. That was four days ago, and he still hasn't spoken to me! When I ask him what's wrong, he says in a curt tone of voice, "Nothing!"

The rerouting of Jim's anger didn't stop there. When his wife called the family to the dinner table, he went to his computer. When she packed him lunches to take to work, he left them in the refrigerator. In turn, she fed them to the dogs just to get back at him. In his anger, Jim stonewalled, and nothing got solved. Just the opposite occurred: The cold war between them intensified with each passing day. When Jim wasn't ranting, raving, or exploding, he was converting his anger into hostile acts that hurt the most important people in his life.

I remember hearing a story about Tommy Bolt, often described as the angriest golfer in the history of the game. He was giving a lesson to a group of golfers, teaching them how to hit a ball out of a sand trap. He called his eleven-year-old son over to him and said, "Show the people what your father has taught you to do when your shot lands in the sand." The young boy picked up a golf club and threw it as hard and as far as his little arm would let him. He had obviously learned his lessons well.

Some of us know we have a problem with anger because it's too conspicuous for anyone to miss. We raise our voice, yell, turn red in the face, cry, curse, throw things, slam doors, or become violent or verbally abusive. Others disguise their anger so that it seems subtler and more socially acceptable. Dr. Willard Gaylan, professor of psychiatry at Columbia University's College of Physicians and Surgeons, wrote a book entitled *The Rage Within: Anger in Modern Life.* In it he says that some of the angriest people have learned to disguise their rage so well that they aren't even aware they're losing their temper.[2]

Even if we don't blow our lids or stuff our feelings, we might sulk, stew, or rehearse what we'd like to say to someone and brood about the one who "hurt" us. We might pull in, withdraw into self-pity or self-critical thoughts, give people the silent treatment, become more controlling, or withhold our love. Or we might use sarcasm and cutting humor, bad-mouth people behind their backs, and recruit people to side with us against others. An even more subtle form of anger is when we hear that something bad has happened to another and yet have no sympathy for them. We may, in fact, even feel a bit happy. This lack of empathy is an indication of anger.

If the way we express our anger is a learned behavior, the good news is that it can be unlearned. A new behavior can take its place. John and I wouldn't be counselors unless we were fully convinced that people can change. God doesn't play favorites. If He will help us with our anger problems, He will help you.

A good way to start is by recognizing our anger style. After that we need to ask a very important question: Do circumstances and other people make us angry, or do we make ourselves angry? We'll answer that question in the next chapter.

Hot tempers start fights;

a calm, cool spirit keeps the peace.

Proverbs 15:18, *The Message*

Chapter Three

Recite the ABCs of Anger

If you are pained by an external thing,

it is not this thing that disturbs you—

but your judgment about it.

MARCUS AURELIUS

HAVE YOU EVER HEARD PEOPLE MAKE STATEMENTS LIKE THESE?

"He makes me so mad!"

"She infuriates me!"

"My kids are driving me crazy!"

"If it weren't for so and so, I wouldn't have blown my cool!"

Have you ever said something similar? If we're honest, most of us have to admit that we occasionally point to someone else as the cause of our anger. There's one big problem with that idea: We can't control our anger as long as we believe that others cause it. We have to take responsibility for fueling the fires that rage within, as well as for dousing them. As long as we believe that the cause of our anger is outside ourselves, we will never be able to master it.

We can't control our anger as long

as we believe that others cause it.

John has a favorite line that he asks his class members to repeat throughout his course: "The truth is: I make me mad." He drives the point home by regularly reiterating: "My wife doesn't make me mad. My kids don't make me mad. My boss doesn't make me mad. My coworkers don't make me mad. The guy who cuts me off on the freeway doesn't make me mad. *I make me mad!*

"I'll say it again: *I make me mad!*"

People, as well as situations and events, can trigger our thoughts and beliefs about something, which can, in turn, make us angry. But in most cases they do not cause our anger. It's what we think and tell ourselves about that person, situation, or event that fuels it.

Dr. Albert Ellis, a pioneer of cognitive behavioral therapy, contends that "crooked thinking" plays a key part in creating emotional conflicts. He says that it's important to look at the ABCs of anger—the events and thoughts that precede the emotion—because the more we understand the irrational things we say to ourselves when we're angry, the better we'll be able to properly process and control our feelings.[1] John and I have found the ABC tool powerful and effective in helping people who are troubled by their anger.

We are what we think. And what we think leads to feelings. Some thoughts make us happy; some make us sad. Others make us angry. The beauty of the ABC tool is that it underscores the fact that we can change our emotional responses to situations by changing what we tell ourselves. This gives us an enormous amount of control over what we feel and do. Let's look at it in detail and trace the chain reaction that leads to anger.

A stands for the *activating* event, or the assumed cause of our anger. This could be any number of things: getting a flat tire on the way to work, not getting the promotion you wanted, a sales clerk hovering when you want to be left alone, someone you've made plans with backing out at the last minute, or your children doing precisely what you've asked them not to. An activating event can also be a thought about the past or the future that concerns you. For example, when I remember the moment we received word from the doctor that our son Nathan had been born with Down's syndrome, the memory serves as an activating event. It triggers thoughts that in turn trigger feelings. The *external* activating event triggers our *internal* thoughts and beliefs.

B stands for our *beliefs* and the things we tell ourselves about the activating events. Some of our beliefs are rational. They help us cope, manage, adjust, and turn down the heat. Other beliefs are irrational, or "crooked." They are not helpful and can actually perpetuate our distress.

C stands for the *consequences* that result from our beliefs and what we say to ourselves. Our internal dialogue evokes a wide array of emotions, one of which can be anger. The various ways we express our anger through our behavior can also be viewed as consequences.

I recently talked with Larry and Karen, who have been married a little over two years. Both are young, full-time graduate school students deeply devoted to their respective fields of study. Wanting to maintain a strong marriage, they had set aside Wednesday night as date night, a time to just be alone together and have fun. But when it was time to register for classes for the second semester of the school year, Larry signed up for one held on Monday and Wednesday nights from 6:00 to 9:00 P.M.

When Karen heard about it, she was livid—so angry that she didn't speak to him for two days. She believed that her anger was due to the fact that Larry had reneged on his commitment to their date night. In other words, she believed that *A*, the activating event (Larry's schedule change), caused *C*, the consequence (her anger and silent withdrawal).

I introduced the ABC tool into the counseling session and asked Karen to think about the *B* in the equation. Bright and insightful, she easily identified what she believed about Larry's schedule change:

His classes are more important than I am.

He doesn't care about our marriage as much as he used to.

Our date night must not matter to him.

If he bails on this, what else is he going to bail on?

These beliefs fueled Karen's anger. She thought they were true. When she and Larry entered my office, I could feel the wall of ice between them. As the counseling session progressed and both expressed their views, it became evident that Karen was caught in the trap of crooked thinking. But once she heard the rationale behind Larry's actions, her beliefs changed and her anger subsided.

Larry made it clear to Karen that date nights were a top priority and that he had planned to talk with her about switching "their" night to Friday, since she didn't have any other commitments that night. Friday was the night he usually shot hoops with a couple of friends down at the local gym, but he was planning to give that up in order to be with her. Karen also learned that the class Larry had signed up for was a required course that was offered only once a year. If he didn't take the class that semester, he wouldn't graduate when he expected to. With this new information, Karen's beliefs changed. Now she believed:

Larry does care about our marriage.

Our date nights do matter to him.

He never intended to bail on me.

His willingness to give up basketball on Fridays shows how much he loves me.

As a result of her new beliefs, Karen's feelings toward Larry went from cold and guarded to warm and fuzzy.

The facts of the situation had not determined how Karen felt; her perception of the facts had evoked the negative emotion. Her beliefs about Larry's choices turned out to be quite different from the actual reasons for them. Once she gave him a chance to share his thoughts with her, she realized that her assumptions were faulty. When the new beliefs replaced the old beliefs, the anger went away.

The important thing to remember about the ABCs is that we don't get from *A* to *C* without going through *B*. Understanding the nature of our beliefs—knowing whether they are rational or irrational—is a big part of properly processing our anger. Anger doesn't have to be an overpowering or unmanageable part of our personality. As we change our thinking, we can change our emotions.

In his extensive years of research and clinical practice, Dr. Ellis identified several distorted beliefs that are commonly held by emotionally disturbed people. If you hang on to any of these twisted beliefs, you will most likely struggle with frequent and intense feelings of anger:

- I must be liked or loved by everyone.
- I must be an expert at everything in order to be worthwhile.
- I have no control over my own happiness. My feelings are caused by what happens to me.
- It's easier to avoid facing life's difficulties and responsibilities than it is to face them.
- It's absolutely awful if things don't turn out the way I want them to.
- There's a right and perfect solution to all problems, and it's bad if I can't find it.
- I must experience pleasure rather than pain.
- If people don't treat me fairly, they are wicked and deserve punishment.

As you can see, these unrealistic expectations can easily ignite anger. There is no possible way that everyone will like us, or that we can be experts at everything we do. Human beings are fallible creatures who exist in imperfect societies, which often don't function according to fair rules. We set ourselves up for anger and emotional disturbances when we convince ourselves that we have a right to expect these things. If these crooked beliefs are rooted in our minds, we will not experience peace and contentment. However, when we realize that they are absurd and replace them with rational thoughts, we can turn down the heat of the fires that rage within.

Did you notice how many *musts* there are in crooked thinking? We want to be on the lookout for any thoughts that include an absolute, such as *must, should, ought,* or *have to.*

Thoughts like *I must...* or *You should...* or *They ought to...* put intense pressure on us, on others, and on the situations we're facing. They trigger frustration and anger.

We can easily upset others and ourselves by thinking that things have to be exactly the way we want them to be. An irritated mother fumes, *My kids must clean up their rooms this minute!* A frustrated businessman insists, *I have to get this order nailed down by this afternoon.* An angry driver thinks, *The guy in front of me should either learn how to drive or get off the road!* An unhappy college student repeatedly tells herself, *I have to pledge that sorority in order to be happy.* A young woman in a bad situation prays over and over, *God, You should have stopped this from happening to me.* Thoughts fraught with *oughts* and *shoulds* energize anger. The more we turn up the demands, the more we fan our emotional flames.

Thoughts fraught with oughts and shoulds energize anger.

Besides erasing the *musts*, *shoulds*, and *oughts* from our internal dialogue, it's important to avoid thoughts that in one way or another say, *This is so terrible that I can't stand it!* A comment like this simply generates more anger and makes us less effective in problem solving. A more rational way to think about our distress is to tell ourselves, *I don't like this situation or feeling angry, but I can tolerate it. I can manage to live a good life in spite of this frustration. God promises to give me the strength to endure what-*

ever comes my way. He also promises to give me the wisdom I need to straighten out my crooked thinking. With His help and some time and effort, I will become more skilled in processing my thoughts and letting my anger go.

The majority of us recognize the necessity of receiving the Holy Spirit for living, but we do not sufficiently recognize the need for drawing on the resources of the Holy Spirit for thinking.

OSWALD CHAMBERS

Chapter Four

Remain Calm

A fool gives full vent to his anger,

but a wise man keeps himself under control.

PROVERBS 29:11

WHEN JOHN AND I COUNSEL PEOPLE STRUGGLING WITH anger, one of the quick tips we offer them is the PPP strategy. It's a fast way to help you remain calm when you feel as though your anger is escalating to a potentially dangerous level. PPP stands for three action steps: Pause. Ponder. Pray.

Stop! The first step in this strategy is to deliberately *pause* to decrease the arousal and buy yourself some time. Allow your body and emotions to cool down before you take action. You may even want to physically leave the situation you're in. If you don't, things can quickly go from bad to worse.

Have you ever noticed that the angrier we get, the dumber we get? When we're angry, the greatest favor we can do for others and ourselves is to pause. Whenever anyone in our family feels that a conversation isn't productive or that the anger of one or more of us is beginning to escalate, we use the referee's "T" sign to call for a time-out. We do this without apology or explanation, knowing that it will keep us all from saying and doing things we would later regret.

Once someone signals for a time-out, we all go our separate ways, knowing that we will come back to the issue at a later time. In ideal situations we make that time an hour, but depending on the issue and our schedules, further discussion may need to wait until another day. The pause is not a maneuver to punish, reject, hurt, or abandon those with whom we are upset. The point is to give us time to calm down.

A quick-tempered man does foolish things.

PROVERBS 14:17

When we're angry about something, our bodies become very tense. Tension is energy swirling at high speed, and according to the laws of nature, energy will always strive to be discharged. If we don't purposely open a release valve and let some of it out, we can become like a pressure cooker on the verge of exploding. But if we pause, we give ourselves a chance to release some of that pent-up energy. Go for a walk or take a long bath. But don't drive. And by all means, do not drink—that will only make matters worse!

Here are some other activities that can stop the escalation of anger and serve as release valves to reduce tension and trigger a relaxation response in your body:

- Take in a deep breath, count to five, and then let it out and relax.
- Tune in to your body and deliberately relax whatever is tense.
- Walk around the room and shake out the tension.
- Get a drink of water.

- Lean back in your chair in a relaxed posture.
- Roll your shoulders and neck.
- Repeat several times: "My body feels calm and relaxed."
- Massage the back of your neck and shoulders.
- Warm a heating pad and place it on your shoulders or lower back.

The second part of the PPP strategy is to *ponder.* We need to ask ourselves what is driving our feelings of frustration and anger. Self-awareness is an important key to managing anger because it allows us to monitor tension and effectively release it. People who are very skilled in managing their anger do this almost intuitively. They have a keen awareness of what is bugging them, and they turn down the heat on their anger so that it doesn't burn them up inside or boil over onto others.

Calm individuals turn down the heat on their anger so that it doesn't burn them up inside or boil over onto others.

Many of these people have learned how to remain calm by using "cool" words instead of "hot" words to talk to themselves about their situation. This calming strategy has tremendous power to reduce arousal, soothe our spirits, and help us cope in the heat of the moment.

Anger doesn't have to escalate. Through the years, John has collected calming statements, which he calls "cool talk," from participants in his classes. These are comments people make to themselves to help them de-escalate when they are angry. We can use them at any time during the course of any interaction, and the more we do, the less likely our anger will blaze out of control. The reverse is also true. The hotter our words, whether thought or spoken, the less likely we'll remain calm. Cool words can keep us in check and prevent us from fueling destructive anger. Here are some examples of cool talk. See which ones work for you.

Cool things to tell yourself when you're angry with someone:

- *Getting angry won't get me what I want in the long run.*
- *Think straight. Keep focused. Stay positive.*
- *Keep reason and respect number one.*
- *Don't blame; look for solutions.*
- *Try to understand his point of view.*
- *This situation isn't worth a coronary.*
- *This problem is annoying, but it doesn't have to be a big deal.*
- *I can look for the humor in this situation.*
- *Conflict is a part of life. I can handle it.*
- *I don't have to take this personally.*
- *What seems so significant today won't seem so a few months from now.*
- *I can pick my fights and save my energies for the more important issues.*
- *Lighten up…you're taking things way too seriously.*
- *God will help us work this out.*

Being in the presence of someone who is angry can be scary and trigger the fight/flight response in us. If we respond with defensive anger, we only add fuel to the fire. But there is a healthier choice: We can disengage and distance ourselves from the person who is shooting fiery darts. By stepping back, we emotionally insulate ourselves from their heat and protect ourselves from getting hooked into an angry sparring match. Cool talk like this can help us create that distance.

COOL THINGS TO TELL YOURSELF WHEN SOMEONE IS ANGRY WITH YOU:

- *Just because he's angry doesn't mean I have to get angry.*
- *Look at all that energy she's wasting.*
- *Even if I don't agree with him, I can listen respectfully.*
- *Try to understand what's driving her anger.*
- *He's way out of control. No need to join him.*
- *It's not up to me to convince her of anything.*
- *I refuse to let him get to me. I have no energy to spare on this.*
- *I've lost my cool before too. I can give her grace.*
- *I don't like his anger, but I can deal with it.*
- *Even if she doesn't like me, I know that God and others do.*
- *Speak softly to turn away his wrath.*
- *Someone needs to help her learn how to manage her anger.*
- *As long as I maintain self-control, I'm doing what's important.*
- *He doesn't have the final say in my life; God does.*

The third part of the PPP strategy is to *pray*. When we tell God all about our hurt and our anger, we do it for our sake, not His. He already knows the secrets of our hearts anyway. I'm not talking about prayers consisting of fancy, pious, religious words. I'm talking about authentically sharing our thoughts and feelings with God as we would with our safest and most trusted friend. Some of the best prayers have more feelings than words. Whispers in the dark, cries from a lonely heart, sighs of confusion, and fumbling utterances offered to God will find their way to His ears, and He will answer.

I want to share a story that highlights the third part of the PPP strategy. I witnessed a transformation in Kim as she prayed her way through a deep hurt that she didn't deserve. I'll let her tell you the story.

For sixteen years after I completed my MBA at Harvard, I was the only woman among the eight vice presidents of a successful corporation. I believed that God had opened the door for me to be there and that He had given me the education and experience I needed to succeed. I loved my job and the people I worked with, and I planned to stay with the firm until I retired.

One afternoon the CEO called me into his office. He spoke enthusiastically about my bright future with the corporation and told me that he saw bigger and better things ahead for me. As I listened, I became very excited about the new opportunities for growth and service that seemed to be opening up for me. Although he didn't go into detail about what my new job would be, he asked me to prepare for it by training two of the people I supervised so they could assume my current responsibilities.

When I finished training them six weeks later, the CEO again called me in for a meeting. Since I was expecting him to talk about my new duties, I was stunned when he told me that my position had been eliminated.

"It's nothing personal," he said. "It's just that we've terminated the position. But there's another in-house position that's open, and you're welcome to that."

That job paid half of what I made as a vice president and required me to report to a man in his twenties who had just graduated from college. Although I was barely able to comprehend what was happening, one thing was clear: The CEO wanted to get rid of me. I resigned, and for months afterward, my anger burned at my boss for his betrayal.

I couldn't sleep. Thoughts of the way he had treated me invaded my dreams or kept me awake heaving huge sighs of frustration. I pictured him losing his job in a hostile takeover or being publicly exposed. The longer I held on to my anger, the fewer good things I could find to say about him. My anger was so deep and pervasive that I was becoming the exact opposite of the person I wanted to be. It was also hurting me much more than it was my boss, and I knew that I had to find a way to let it go and get on with my life.

But how?

One thing was clear: I couldn't do it alone. I needed God's help, and I began to talk to Him about my feelings day and night. As angry as I was, listening to what He was saying to me was more difficult, but even so, it soon became clear to me that He was prompting me to do a few things.

When I found myself obsessed with memories of the injustice, I pictured myself writing down all the events on a huge blackboard. Then, after I recorded all of the things that my mind wouldn't let go of, I picked up a big eraser, wiped the board clean, and told God that I couldn't carry these thoughts around in my head any longer. They were His to handle now, not mine.

I don't typically keep a journal, but during that difficult time, I somehow felt the need to register my concerns with God in a concrete way. At first I felt embarrassed to write about my hurt and anger because it seemed like I was whining, but after journaling for a while, I began to feel emotional relief. It also brought clarity by giving me added perspective. After a time, I could reread what I'd written earlier and realize that I didn't feel quite as angry anymore.

The more I journaled, the more I found myself recording insights from Scripture that seemed to apply directly to my situation. When I came across a verse that spoke to my circumstances, I saw it as a promise from God, and I tried my best to *act* like I believed it. That helped me to focus on God and today, instead of on my boss and the past. One of the verses that helped me the most was: "God is not unjust; he will not forget your work and the love you have shown him as you have helped his people and continue to help them" (Hebrews 6:10).

That verse gave me the confidence I needed to start over. I knew that I wanted to continue to help people and to love them as I had the people I'd worked with for so many years. So, after giving myself time to weigh the alternatives, I decided to become a freelance consultant. Committing myself to this new venture was another big step in the healing process.

Even so, it took almost a year for my anger to completely subside. And that doesn't mean I don't still feel the pain of the wound now and then, because I do. But the anger doesn't control me. Obsessing over the wrong doesn't dominate my thoughts or rule my life. As I look back now, I can see that when I took my turmoil to God in prayer, He was faithful to help me by showing me some specific and creative ways to let my anger go.

In the midst of the pain and confusion that accompany situations in which we struggle with anger, we need to pause, ponder, and pray. We need to turn to God and say, *God, I need Your help. Give me Your perspective. Let my eyes see as You see. Let my heart hear Your heart. Grant me insight into what You are doing in my life right now. Show me what I need to do to cooperate with You in letting my anger go.* And then we need to pay very close attention to the whisperings of the Holy Spirit and be mindful of the insights that bubble to the surface.

Because God will be faithful to answer those kinds of prayers.

Is anyone among you suffering?
Then he must pray. The effective prayer of a
righteous man can accomplish much.

James 5:13, 16, NASB

Chapter Five

Relinquish Control

The greatness of a man's power

is the measure of his surrender.

William Booth

"I just don't get it!" Bob exclaimed. "When my boss gives me an assignment, I find myself eager to work long hours and do a top-notch job. But if he gives me a task and then goes on and on about every little detail involved, I start feeling resistant—like I want to tune him out." Confused by his conflicting feelings, Bob had come to John for help.

"When your boss is giving you a long list of instructions, do you feel angry?" John asked.

"I don't know if it's anger or not," Bob replied. "It just feels as though he's trying to micromanage my job."

"Sounds like you don't like feeling micromanaged," John observed.

"You've got that right! I was hired to do a job, and I wish he'd just let me do it. He has this thing about everything having to be done his way. But what about my own creativity? I have some great things to offer his business if he'd just give me some breathing room."

John probed further. "Bob, can you remember times in your past when you felt like this?"

"Oh, sure—when I was a kid. There was a lot of tension

in my house. My dad was an Army man. His word was law. We were all expected to obey him, no questions asked. I could never talk frankly about things that bothered me. If I had a complaint, Dad told me not to be a wimp and then shut me out. I remember when I wanted to take computer classes in junior high. He laughed it off and said that kind of stuff was for sissies. He wanted to control everything I did. There were times when I wanted to deck the guy." Bob took a deep breath, sighed in distress, and looked at the floor.

"It sounds as if your anger was simply a cry of protest against a very rigid environment," John remarked. "Does your anger with your boss seem similar to the anger you felt with your father?"

Bob paused a moment to think and then replied, "Yes, I suppose it does."

Perhaps you grew up in a rigid environment similar to Bob's, where you lived under a set of dogmatic, unreasonable rules. But even if your background is different, perhaps you can relate to the feelings that surface when you find yourself in situations where others are calling the shots, placing what seem to be unreasonable demands on you, or making decisions that impact you without your input. You might sense that you aren't being given choices or that someone is overtly or covertly manipulating you. You feel controlled...and you feel angry.

That's what happened to Bob. There was a fire smoldering in him, and it was about to burst into flames. But as a thirty-eight-year-old adult, he realized that his anger was self-defeating. He wanted to learn how to respond to his boss's attempts to micromanage him in a way that would extinguish the smoldering coals instead of fanning them into a flame.

Trying to control others creates

a vicious cycle that only generates anger.

The truth is that few of us like being controlled, and when we feel that we are, we usually become angry and resist by trying to reassert our own control. What are some ways we attempt to use control or countercontrol strategies in our relationships?

It's fairly easy to spot overt tactics. They are visible when we are bossy, critical, highly defensive, argumentative, or speak in an intense tone of voice. Reminding, nagging, lecturing, giving unsolicited advice, screaming, begging, bribing, coercing, complaining, whining, insisting, criticizing, pressuring, intimidating, checking up on, forming coalitions, minding other people's business, dropping subtle and not-so-subtle hints, and interrogating are all signs that we are being controlling.

It's a bit harder to detect covert tactics, but they are just as real. They include withdrawing, avoiding, giving the silent treatment, pouting, or treating others with indifference. Some may feign helplessness and try to elicit pity from those around them. Others might hide behind a facade of spirituality and phony religious rhetoric. Whatever the strategy, the underlying goal is always the same: to make people do what we want them to do.

Whether we rely on these tactics to assert control over other people or to counter their attempts to control us, when we resort to them, we find ourselves caught in a vicious cycle that only generates more anger. I witnessed this in my relationship with our daughter one year when she was in high school.

Jessie had suffered an injury that not only sidelined her from a sport she deeply loved, but also led to several months of chronic pain that interrupted her sleep and made it difficult for her to concentrate in class. The stress depressed her immune system, and it seemed as though she caught every virus known to man that year. She missed classes for long stretches of time, and make-up assignments piled high. The academic load of the honors classes she was taking completely overwhelmed her.

Wanting to be a good mom, I moved in to fix things. I scheduled times for us to work together on homework, collected handouts from teachers when Jessie was home sick, told her I would proofread her papers (after all, writing is my thing), offered to hire tutors (her advanced math classes were beyond John and me), talked with the school counselor, and did what I could do to help out.

There was one problem: Jessie didn't want me to fix things. She hadn't asked for my help, and she really wasn't interested in it. Actually, it was worse than that. She saw my efforts to help not as support, but as pressure, and she flat-out resented it.

Of course, I was "only trying to help." I wanted to do my job as a responsible parent and make sure she was doing what she was supposed to do. I saw the bigger picture, knew things needed to change, and was bound and determined to change them. I tried all the positive reinforcement and bargaining strategies in the book, and sad to say, I ended up making both of us miserable…and angry.

One afternoon I spoke with my mentor and told her about the frustration I felt about Jessie being behind in school. She had always been an honors student. This was new territory we hadn't traveled before, and it was scary. Wise woman that she is, my mentor said, "Your daughter is very bright. She isn't the kind of person who is going to do something simply because you think it's a good idea. She'll do something about this when she concludes for herself that it's a good idea. Even then, she may not want your help. Your efforts to 'help' are driving her away. Which is more important, your relationship with your daughter, or your daughter's grades?"

Ouch.

Nailed to the wall.

I realized that I had spent more time and energy trying to manage Jessie's academic performance than being sensitive to her more pressing personal needs. In her difficult time of loss, she needed more of my listening ear and less of my unsolicited advice.

Shortly after meeting with my mentor, I unloaded the burdens of my heart to God. I talked about my confusion as a mom and asked Him if I was doing too much, enough, or not enough to support Jessie. I wanted to find a healthy balance. His answer surprised me. In my mind I saw a big toolbox, brimming over with dozens of tools. Big tools. Little tools. Sharp ones. Dull ones. Straight. Crooked. Rough. Smooth. Every kind of tool imaginable. I sensed that the Lord wanted to impress me with this message: *You are only one tool in this toolbox. I am using many other tools to shape Jessie.*

I finally got the message: I needed to stop trying so hard and surrender Jessie to God. My control strategies were preventing me from loving and enjoying her as God desired. God was very aware of what was going on in her life, and He knew that her situation didn't require me to assert control as a part of discipline. In a kind way, He asked me to step aside so that He could continue the good work He had begun in her. I did.

When the new school year began, Jessie discovered other activities she enjoyed and set some academic goals for herself. Because they were her decisions, things went much better. Both of us felt much less anger, and love flowed more freely between us. Releasing my grip on her freed both of us and allowed our lives to unfold more naturally.

When we think we can control others, we're only fooling ourselves. Eventually people will either resist our efforts, or they will redouble their own efforts to make the point that they will not be controlled. Nothing changes, and everyone ends up angry. If we take it upon ourselves to try to control others in order to get our own way, we will find ourselves irritable, agitated, hot tempered, and, ultimately, out of control. Paul sums it up nicely:

> It is obvious what kind of life develops out of *trying to get your own way all the time:* repetitive, loveless, cheap sex; a stinking accumulation of mental and emotional garbage; frenzied and joyless grabs for happiness; trinket gods;

> magic-show religion; paranoid loneliness; cutthroat competition; all-consuming-yet-never-satisfied wants; *a brutal temper*; *an impotence to love or be loved;* divided homes and divided lives; small-minded and lopsided pursuits; the vicious habit of depersonalizing everyone into a rival; *uncontrolled and uncontrollable* addictions; ugly parodies of community. I could go on.

Galatians 5:19–21, *The Message*, emphasis added

We can make a better choice: We can bring our focus back to our own lives and concentrate on living life God's way. As Paul indicates, the results are far more rewarding:

> But what happens when we live God's way? He brings gifts into our lives, much the same way that fruit appears in an orchard—things like affection for others, exuberance about life, serenity. We develop a willingness to stick with things, a sense of compassion in the heart, and a conviction that a basic holiness permeates things and people. We find ourselves involved in loyal commitments, *not needing to force our way in life, able to marshal and direct our energies wisely....* Among those who belong to Christ, everything connected with *getting our own way* and mindlessly responding to what everyone else calls necessities is killed off for good—crucified.
>
> Since this is the kind of life we have

> chosen, the life of the Spirit, let us make sure that we do not just hold it as an idea in our heads or a sentiment in our hearts, but work out its implications in every detail of our lives. That means we will not compare ourselves with each other as if one of us were better and another worse. We have far more interesting things to do with our lives. Each of us is an original.
>
> GALATIANS 5:22–26, *THE MESSAGE*, EMPHASIS ADDED

Notice how Paul makes the point that each person is unique? I have my place in this world, and you have yours. God doesn't ask me to carry out your assignments, and He doesn't ask you to carry out mine. Uniqueness necessitates differences. We need to focus on living the original, unique plan God designed for us, and we need to allow others the freedom to do the same.

Nowhere in the Bible are we told to try to control others. Nowhere does God instruct us to force what we think is best on them. The truth is that the only person God asks us to control is ourself. We aren't to try to make others over in our image. The world doesn't need another John or Pam Vredevelt. It doesn't need another, _______________(fill in your name). But it does need people who are living God's way, daily being changed by the Holy Spirit to reflect God's image.

Nowhere in the Bible are

we told to try to control others.

When Jesus was asked which was the greatest commandment, He replied: "'Love the Lord your God with all your passion and prayer and intelligence.' This is the most important, the first on any list. But there is a second to set alongside it: 'Love others as well as you love yourself'" (Matthew 22:39, *The Message*).

Note that the commandment that follows right on the heels of the first is *not* "Control others as you control yourself." We love others when we give them the freedom to make choices and learn from their mistakes and successes, free from our attempts to control them. It's the way God loves us, and it's the way He wants us to love others.

How do we let go of anger? We open our clenched fists and relinquish control. We turn things loose. We resist the temptation to play God and allow Him to reign without a rival.

An infant is born with a clenched fist,

but an old man dies with an open hand.

Life has a way of prying loose our grasp

on all that seems so important.

Anonymous

Chapter Six

Resolve Unmet Needs

And my God will meet all your needs according to his glorious riches in Christ Jesus.

PHILIPPIANS 4:19

CATHY, WHOSE HUSBAND, MATT, WAS COUNSELING WITH John, requested an appointment with me to discuss some things that were troubling her. This couple had a daughter who was born with Down's syndrome, and I thought Cathy might want to focus on issues pertaining to her. My assumption was wrong: She was so angry with Matt that she was entertaining the idea of divorce.

At first glance, Cathy seemed to have a great life. Matt was a very successful businessman who provided her with many luxuries, including a big home in a lovely part of town. She enjoyed living in beautiful surroundings, and his substantial income allowed her to decorate their home as she wanted.

Cathy had always wanted to be a stay-at-home mom, and Matt fully supported her desire. Their son was a well-adjusted youngster, a good student and an athlete. Despite her handicap, their daughter functioned very well and was in good health. Although Matt was on the job fifty hours a week, he was with the family most evenings and weekends and was actively involved in the children's lives.

Although Matt was already fulfilling many of her

desires, Cathy was still angry and unhappy. She told me that Matt did not meet her emotional needs and that she longed for a soul mate who would share intimate thoughts and feelings with her.

As Cathy described the man of her dreams, it seemed to me that her ideal lover came straight from the pages of a Harlequin romance. In fact, I later learned that one of her favorite pastimes was reading romance novels. As I listened to her, it occurred to me that her romantic expectations of marriage would never be met, because what she longed for was an unrealistic fantasy fed by Hollywood fairy tales and softcover fiction. The more she nurtured the fantasy, the angrier and more dissatisfied she was with Matt for not meeting her needs.

A persistent diet of romance novels can stir up unrealistic expectations in marriage.

Cathy is not alone. Harlequin Publishers sells hundreds of millions of paperbacks a year. I've had women in therapy tell me that they were hooked on romance novels much like a cocaine addict is hooked on the drug. Now, don't get me wrong: I'm all for curling up with a good book as a diversion from the stresses of life. But a persistent diet of romance novels can stir up unrealistic expectations in marriage and leave women feeling as though their husbands have shortchanged them.

"Cathy, I'd like to ask you a question," I said. "May I?" She nodded her head, giving me the go-ahead.

"Cathy, you have an eight-year-old daughter with Down's syndrome. Do you expect your daughter to be able to do what your son did when he was eight years old?"

"Of course not!" she replied. "She's handicapped. There's no way!"

"So, are you saying that you've adjusted your expectations of her because she's handicapped?" I inquired.

"Well, sure…," she said. "It would be silly not to."

After asking her permission to speak frankly, I said, "It's just about as silly to expect your husband to meet all your emotional needs. There's no way he can. He has some handicaps, just like the rest of the men on this planet. They're not taught how to meet the emotional needs of a woman. They spend much of their emotional energy providing for their families. And when you think about it, women are just as handicapped in their abilities to meet all the needs of a man."

I don't think I told Cathy what she wanted to hear that day, but she thanked me for the time we had together and said she'd think things through. A couple of weeks later she came back to my office toting the book *Men Are From Mars, Women Are From Venus.* She said she wanted to learn more about the differences between men and women. It was a sign to me that she was open to reconsidering her expectations of Matt.

As time passed, Cathy worked on defining her most important needs and communicating them more clearly to Matt. She realized that her way of asking him for closeness was too vague and that it usually ended up sounding like a complaint. Rather than commenting on his lack of attentiveness, she started suggesting that they do some things together that she enjoyed. She also took the initiative to plan quarterly weekend getaways for them so they could focus on each other without all the typical interruptions at home.

Matt wanted the marriage to work, and as he continued his counseling with John, he learned how to be more tuned in and responsive to the things that mattered to Cathy. Having grown up without a father in his home, Matt had to learn these skills in his thirties. In all honesty, he didn't become a flaming romantic, but he did grow in his ability to express thoughtfulness and affection.

One of the most fulfilling choices Cathy made was to start attending a women's group at their church. The new friendships she made there took the pressure off Matt to be the only person meeting her relational needs. Hearing the challenges other women faced in marriage also opened her eyes to Matt's many strengths. Cathy learned to not let her fantasies fuel her expectations of Matt, to be thankful for the needs he was able to meet, and to let go of the anger she had held on to for years.

I want to mention a related fact: Many men who seek counseling for help with anger speak of having, or having had, a problem with pornography or other sexual addictions. One man, who attended John's anger management class as well as a recovery group for sexual addiction, told John that his feelings of anger were as good at covering up his inner conflicts as pornography was. Both created a sort of high that effectively numbed his feelings of loneliness and inadequacy.

That is not surprising, because the chemical release that occurs in the brain in response to sexual stimulation and anger is similar. There is an addictive element to this chemical release because eventually the high of the past no longer satisfies, and a person has to increase the activity to get the same kind of fix.

In *Pure Desire*, Dr. Ted Roberts points out the potential consequences of this kind of addiction:

> Sexual activity and fantasy, which produce the sense of pleasure, can actually alter a person's brain chemistry. This altered brain chemistry is a beautiful experience between a husband and wife. But when it is taken out of this context, it is the "high" not the relationship that becomes the focus. The other person is not important because he or she is simply the object that delivers the fix. This is why a sex addict can pursue seemingly irrational courses of action, such as repeated relationships with women other than his wife, or even prostitutes, despite the fact that he declares that he loves God. He gets a "buzz" from the danger of it.[1]

Intense anger not only gives a similar sort of buzz, but also fuels marital infidelity. In all the years John and I have been counselors, we haven't met anyone who was unfaithful to his or her spouse who didn't have a problem with anger. Sometimes the anger was obvious, but not always. We've met many people in the midst of affairs who were experts at camouflaging their anger or driving it underground. Making choices against your conscience and your personal convictions takes an emotional push, and the emotion that energizes that push is anger.

Sexual immorality and anger are joined at the hip.

I say all of this simply to underline the fact that fantasies, anger, sexual addictions, and infidelity are connected. We often find these issues mentioned together in Scripture. In a letter to the Corinthian church, the apostle Paul says:

> I am afraid that when I come…there may be quarreling, jealousy, outbursts of anger, factions, slander, gossip, arrogance and disorder…and I will be grieved over many who have sinned earlier and have not repented of the impurity, sexual sin and debauchery in which they have indulged.
>
> 2 Corinthians 12:20–21

And in a letter to the church at Colosse, he says this:

> Put to death…whatever belongs to your earthly nature: sexual immorality, impurity, lust…. You used to walk in these ways, in the life you once lived. But now you must rid yourselves of all such things as these: anger, rage, malice, slander, and filthy language from your lips.
>
> Colossians 3:5, 7–8

Sexual immorality and anger are joined at the hip. Often the anger stems from unmet needs either within the marriage or within other significant relationships, past or present. When people allow such needs to continue unattended, they become vulnerable to rationalizing their behavior in a way that allows them to seek instant gratification. Unhealthy choices are driven by angry beliefs like *If so-and-so won't give me what I want, then I'll get it another way, and I don't care if I have to break a few rules to do it.*

Resolving unmet needs can diffuse anger and diminish the likelihood of making other unhealthy choices. Sometimes we can meet these needs by making changes on the outside, or within our environment. Other times we can satisfy them by making changes on the inside, such as revising our expectations. Still, I don't know anyone who feels that all of his or her needs are met all of the time. There are times when this just isn't possible, particularly if the changes we desire involve another person. Like it or not, we cannot force others to change.

The complete fulfillment of our physical, psychological, and spiritual needs will be realized only in heaven. Until then, we will all have some unmet needs, and we need God to help us sort through these challenges. He alone knows when we suffer in silence, confused and conflicted about the empty spaces in our soul. He knows what we're missing. He takes stock of our insufficiencies, and He promises to meet our needs as no one else can.

Henri Nouwen reminded me of this in his book *The Road to Daybreak.* A Catholic priest trained at Yale University, Nouwen held a professorship at Harvard and traveled the world as a renowned author and lecturer. Midway through his career, he left behind prestige and power to serve severely handicapped people in France. In his book, he chronicles his spiritual journey during those years of transition, and in this journal entry he makes it clear that God alone can meet our deepest needs:

> It is hard for me to speak of my feelings of being rejected or imposed upon, of my desire for affirmation as well as my need for space, of insecurity and mistrust, of fear and love. But as I entered into these feelings, I also discovered the real problem—expecting from a friend what only Christ can give....
>
> I learned afresh that friendship requires a constant willingness to forgive each other for not being Christ, and a willingness to ask Christ himself to be the true center. When Christ does not mediate a relationship, that relationship easily becomes demanding, manipulating, oppressive, an arena for many forms of rejection. An unmediated friendship cannot last long; you simply expect too much of the other and cannot offer the other the space he or she needs to grow.[2]

Our family and friends can meet some of our needs, but ultimately, God is the one who is all-sufficient. He has given us His Word. He has promised to give us wisdom. He will enable us to examine our unmet needs, revise unrealistic expectations, and let our anger go. We have only to ask.

Let us then approach the throne

of grace with confidence,

so that we may receive mercy and find grace

to help us in our time of need.

Hebrews 4:16

Chapter Seven

Resist the Pharisee Syndrome

And do not bring sorrow to God's
Holy Spirit by the way you live.
Get rid of all bitterness, rage, anger,
harsh words, and slander,
as well as all types of malicious behavior.

EPHESIANS 4:30–31, NLT

I WAS ANGRY. JOHN AND I HAD HAD AN ARGUMENT THE night before, and I was having a hard time letting go of the ill feelings it had triggered. It was a petty thing. We were scheduled to shoot a video series for married couples on a particular date. He was certain he had told me the date, but I was sure he hadn't. I had told him that an out-of-town guest was coming that weekend, and he had entered his reminder on another weekend. So now we had to reschedule the video shoot, which was embarrassing for us and an inconvenience to the people involved. Neither of us was happy with the other. Someone could have parked a truck in the middle of our king-size bed that night, and we never would have known it. We were both hugging the edges.

Silly, isn't it? Two educated adults, who teach couples how to achieve intimacy in their marriages, end up in a standoff about a scheduling mix-up. Oh, we both had our rational arguments. But I didn't want to hear his, and he didn't want to hear mine. And make no mistake: This time, I wanted him to be the first to say he was sorry. As far as I was concerned, he had made the bigger error.

The Pharisee within me stood tall, refusing to budge an inch.

And the results? Anger. Alienation from my partner in life. Self-deception. And grief to the Spirit of God. That's the power of the Pharisee syndrome. It leads us to believe that we are faultless, or at least less at fault than another. That we know better. That we *are* better. Linked tightly with pride, it's a spiritual disease that drives anger and destroys relationships.

I went back and reread the parable of the Pharisee:

> [Jesus] told his next story to some who were complacently pleased with themselves over their moral performance and looked down their noses at the common people: "Two men went up to the Temple to pray, one a Pharisee, the other a tax man. The Pharisee posed and prayed like this: 'Oh, God, I thank you that I am not like other people—robbers, crooks, adulterers, or, heaven forbid, like this tax man. I fast twice a week and tithe on all my income.'
>
> "Meanwhile the tax man, slumped in the shadows, his face in his hands, not daring to look up, said, 'God, give mercy. Forgive me, a sinner.'"
>
> Jesus commented, "This tax man, not the other, went home made right with God. If you walk around with your nose in the air, you're going to end up flat on your face, but if you're content to be simply yourself, you will become more than yourself."
>
> LUKE 18:9–14, *THE MESSAGE*

I sighed and turned to my Father in heaven: *Well, I guess that about hits the nail on the head, Lord. That's how I feel today—like someone who is flat on my face, without much oomph to get up. Okay, I get the message: I forgive John.*

By the way, my feelings were saying the exact opposite, but I knew I needed to choose to let go of my anger anyway. I knew that if I didn't respond to what God was showing me, things were not going to get better within me or in my relationship with John. I sensed the Holy Spirit's sadness over the hardness of our hearts toward each other. God is love, and anything that isn't love pains Him. A thought crossed my mind: *It is more important to love than to be right.*

It is more important to love than to be right.

So I prayed some more. *Lord, please forgive me for acting like a Pharisee. I detest how I think and act when I play that role. I don't want to be a person who is stubborn, self-willed, and critical. I surrender my need to be right to You and ask You to help John and me make things right between us.*

Then I called John at work and apologized for my part in the conflict. He apologized for his. It wasn't a conversation for a Hallmark commercial. No warm fuzzies were present for either of us. And when I hung up the phone, I was amazed at how unrelenting the Pharisee within me was to make a point. I was still secretly hoping that John had grasped the fact that I was right and he was wrong. My, oh my, pride dies hard!

I'm so glad that God is bigger than my dark side. I'm so

thankful that I'm not alone in my struggle. I think of the candid words Paul spoke to the Romans about his own battles:

> I truly delight in God's commands, but it's pretty obvious that not all of me joins in that delight. Parts of me covertly rebel, and just when I least expect it, they take charge.
>
> I've tried everything and nothing helps. I'm at the end of my rope. Is there no one who can do anything for me? Isn't that the real question?
>
> ROMANS 7:22–24, *THE MESSAGE*

And I find hope in how he responds to the question raised:

> The answer, thank God, is that Jesus Christ can and does. He acted to set things right in this life of contradictions where I want to serve God with all my heart and mind, but am pulled by the influence of sin to do something totally different....
>
> God's Spirit is right alongside helping us along.
>
> ROMANS 7:25; 8:26, *THE MESSAGE*

Just in case you're wondering, the rest of the day wasn't exactly fabulous, but it was a whole lot better. We gave up our attempts to persuade each other and made efforts to repair the breach. John realized that he had overreacted, and I realized that

I had overreacted to his overreaction. It wasn't a fairy-tale ending, but at least we were on the same page! When we went to sleep that night, the anger and the space in the middle of the bed were gone. And so was the Holy Spirit's grief.[1]

When one knows oneself well,

one is not desirous of looking into the faults of others.

I wish I could say that it's easy for me to let go of anger. And I wish I could say that I always trust God—that I never argue, talk back, or demand my own way. But I can't, because at times I find myself doing those very things.

I remember one night when I was rocking Nathan to sleep. My soul was as dark as the night. Nathan was approaching a birthday, and birthdays seem to trigger both joy and grief, even when I try to focus on celebration. We have so much for which to be thankful. But on that particular night I must have been especially worn out, because my "attitude of gratitude" had flown the coop. I was in the middle of a power struggle with God.

I didn't want Nathan to be mentally retarded. I wanted him to be "normal."

I didn't want Nathan to be mute. I longed to hear his thoughts and feelings.

I didn't want Nathan to need special assistance at school and church.

I wanted Nathan to be independent and capable like Jessie and Ben.

Looking back, I think I honestly believed that I knew what was best for Nathan and the rest of us, and it didn't include a diagnosis of Down's syndrome. The Pharisee in me declared: "I want what I want, when I want it!" And I was angry because I hadn't gotten my way.

The Pharisee in me declared:

"I want what I want, when I want it!"

I had been in this place before, struggling with the discrepancy between the ideal and the real. *How,* I wondered, *am I going to plan a fun-filled birthday party for Nathan while I'm in the middle of throwing myself a first-class pity party?* Tears fell, and I rocked Nathan for a long time that evening—more for my sake than his.

During those quiet moments, an unexpected insight came. I sensed God saying, *Pam, I always give you My best.* The truth penetrated the core of my soul, and I wept. God had shone a spotlight on my prideful, stubborn will, and I realized that my resistance to the fact that Nathan was handicapped was the cause of much of my anguish.

Have you ever noticed that resisting circumstances does not change things? What is, is. Wrestling with reality gets us nowhere…except angry. But we can trust that no matter where we are at a particular time in our lives, God wants to give us His best. Resisting the Pharisee syndrome and letting God be God is the first step to accepting our circumstances and letting go of our anger.

For all of us, whatever our circumstance, the realization that "this is not what I want" triggers anger. But we don't always get what we want, and admitting that presents us with a choice. We can act like petulant children. We can argue, resist, slam doors, demand our way, and pout. Or we can surrender to the Lord our God and focus on the truth that He has a good plan for our lives and that His intention is to bless us. We can clench our fists and shake them in angry defiance, or we can open our hands in acceptance and ask God to take what we yield to Him and give us His best.

A passage in the book of Jeremiah can help us put things in perspective:

> The Lord gave another message to Jeremiah. He said, "Go down to the shop where clay pots and jars are made. I will speak to you while you are there." So I did as he told me and found the potter working at his wheel. But the jar he was making did not turn out as he had hoped, so the potter squashed the jar into a lump of clay and started again.
>
> Then the Lord gave me this message: "O Israel, can I not do to you as this potter has done to his clay? As the clay is in the potter's hand, so are you in my hand."
>
> 18:1–6, NLT

Hard things happen in this world. No one warned us that this particular phase of the journey would be this dark. Yet as we dwell in the Potter's hands, even though we may be confused, in pain, and angry, we can trust that God is at work shaping us. For what? For what Paul called His "noble purposes." In pure faith we can rest, knowing that His intentions are good and that His direction is strategic. He is transforming us into His image. He's removing impurities and refining us like gold. It's our job to be pliable in His strong and tender hands.

We can trust that God cares about what we hold dear to our hearts. In time, more clarity will come. He really can make all things work together for our best—even the strange, unplanned situations that blindside us and tempt us to lash out in anger. We can trust that in the years ahead, we will look back on today's painful circumstances and see how God used them to shape us into vessels worthy of honor. Even our worst mistakes can become springboards that launch us into divine assignments.

That dark night as I sat rocking Nathan, my divine assignment was to make a holy exchange: my anger, pride, and pharisaical demands for God's assurance that the potter was at work. I needed to become less childish and more childlike—like Nathan, relaxed, sleeping soundly in my arms, confident that all was well.[2]

If we want to let go of our anger,
we must quit playing judge and jury
and accept the limits and imperfections
we see in ourselves and others.

Chapter Eight

Rest and Renew

If you don't slow down, you'll break down.

JUDITH ST. PIERRE

TODD, A FORTY-YEAR-OLD SUCCESSFUL CORPORATE EXECUTIVE, scheduled an appointment with John because he wanted to learn how to manage his anger. Todd's job had kept him driving himself at maximum speed for long hours, day after day, for years. By the time he sought counseling, he was living on the verge of burnout. He complained of fatigue and depression. He felt that life wasn't worth living, and he was sick and tired of being sick and tired. "I work sixty hours a week and have never been more frustrated in all my life," he told John. "Everywhere I turn I have to put out another fire. If it's not one thing, it's another." He also complained of feeling irritable all the time.

Make no mistake: Overworked, stressed-out people are angry! They may not show it, but the chronic unmet need for rest and renewal steals their joy and leaves them feeling resentful. It's impossible to have sound physical, mental, and spiritual health if we deprive our bodies and ignore our basic needs. Making his job his highest priority had gradually destroyed any balance Todd might have had in his life and had left him feeling angry.

In a typical day, Todd's alarm went off at 5:00 in the

morning, he was on his way to work by 6:00, and he seldom walked back through the door at the end of the day before 7:30. After grabbing a quick bite to eat, he spent a few hours catching up on deskwork and reading e-mails before turning out the lights at 11:00. When John asked Todd how he was able to stay awake at the office after only six hours sleep, he replied, "That's all the sleep anybody gets in my line of work. We just keep the coffee going all day...."

For fast-acting relief, try slowing down.

I hear the same complaints from many top-level professionals, but they are not alone. It's a common dilemma. We live in a very fast-paced world that places heavy demands on us. Our daily planners are crammed with entries marked Action Required, and there are never enough hours in a day to accomplish everything on our to-do lists. And while this is true, we need to remember that sleep is one of the primary ways the body restores itself. If we rob ourselves of sleep by burning the candle at both ends, we will be irritable and easily angered.

Studies on sleep deprivation show that sleep is necessary for our brain to work efficiently, especially the higher-level brain processes that sustain focused attention, concentration, and motivation. During World War II, some of our prisoners of war were deprived of sleep as a form of torture. Whenever they fell asleep, their captors immediately awakened them. As this treatment continued, the prisoners became extremely anxious, irritable, confused, and impulsive. Under these intensely stressful conditions, a few of them revealed military information that they would have concealed had they been able to renew their brain processes through sleep. There is no question that a consistent pattern of sound sleep increases our ability to successfully manage the various stresses we experience in life.

It is also common knowledge that people who try to live on less than four or five hours of sleep for an ongoing period of time are at higher risk for dying. By living in 911 mode during most of his waking hours and not getting enough sleep at night, Todd was setting himself up for a stroke or heart attack. The human body will endure extreme pressure only so long before it starts sending overload messages. Todd's perpetual irritability and depression were clear signs that the brain chemicals responsible for sustaining a good mood and clarity of thought were being severely taxed.

People who cannot find time for recreation are obliged sooner or later to find time for illness.

JOHN WANAMAKER

One of John's goals was to help Todd find a balance between fulfilling the demands of his job and meeting his physical needs. He encouraged Todd to give himself permission to take care of his body not only by getting enough sleep, but also by routinely setting aside periods of time for exercise to reduce his stress.

Todd set small, incremental goals and gradually incorporated them into his daily routine. He began by setting limits on the number of hours he spent at the office so he could use the company's exercise facility after work. Instead of leaving the office at 7:00 P.M., he left somewhere between 5:00 and 6:00 in order to work out with weights, jog on the treadmill for thirty minutes, and shower before heading home. He tried to do this a minimum of three times a week.

If his day had been particularly stressful, on the drive home he listened to a relaxing instrumental CD instead of the usual talk show. He reduced the time he spent on deskwork and the Internet after dinner and made an effort to be in bed by 9:30 P.M., which made it possible for him to get seven and one-half hours of sleep before the alarm sounded at 5:00 A.M.

It is our best work that God wants,
not the dregs of our exhaustion.
I think he must prefer quality to quantity.

GEORGE MACDONALD

After several weeks of this new routine, Todd said that his energy level had increased, but he still complained that he felt depressed and irritable much of the time. In reviewing Todd's family history, John discovered that Todd's father and grandfather had also struggled with depression. He talked with Todd about the possibility that he had a genetic predisposition for depression, which for some people feels more like perpetual irritability and anger than a blue mood. At John's suggestion,

Todd saw his physician, who prescribed an antidepressant for Todd to use for six to nine months.

The brain is like any other organ in the body: It can become impaired and not function properly for any of a number of reasons. We know that prolonged periods of stress can deplete the chemicals in the brain responsible for good mood, concentration, focus, motivation, sound sleep, and overall peace of mind. Medications such as the antidepressant that Todd's doctor prescribed work on the brain like a cast or splint would work on a broken arm. They support the brain's nerve cells while a person is learning new, stress-reducing habits, and they enhance healing by bolstering the brain chemicals depleted by chronic stress.

John and I have heard people express fears about using antidepressant medicines. Some are concerned about becoming addicted; others fear that it will change their personality. These are unfounded fears that perpetuate unnecessary suffering. When medications are judiciously and appropriately applied—not one size fits all—people can recover from depression. Research shows that the majority of people treated with a combination of medication and cognitive behavior therapy experience marked improvement and relief. On the average, one-third of those taking medication can discontinue its use within nine to twelve months, another third will need to use it intermittently through life, and another third will benefit from ongoing use.

Let's go back to Todd and John. The first antidepressant Todd tried was overly sedating and caused some nausea, so the doctor prescribed a second medication, which ended up being just the right fit. Within a month, Todd's mood and motivation were much improved, and he was able to be more objective and less reactive on the job. Little problems didn't instantaneously become big problems in his mind as they had previously.

So here's what I want you to do,
God helping you:
Take your everyday, ordinary life—
your sleeping, eating, going-to-work,
and walking-around life—
and place it before God as an offering.

ROMANS 12:1, *THE MESSAGE*

Todd's conscientious attention to his physical needs played an important role in his ability to overcome his pervasive irritability and anger. But John's work with Todd didn't stop with these basic strategies for physical self-care. He wanted to help Todd address his unmet spiritual needs, which were helping fuel the workaholic tendencies that resulted in his chronic fatigue and anger.

Todd had been so busy with work that he hadn't left time for his relationship with God. "I stopped going to church because I wanted to do things around the house on Sunday that I couldn't get done during the week," he told John.

"What kind of an impact has that choice had on you?" John asked.

After pausing to think, Todd replied, "It's left me feeling disconnected from God."

"Todd, you came in for counseling wanting to learn how to manage your anger. You're feeling better now because you're taking care of your physical needs. But your spiritual needs are equally important. Our frustration decreases and our peace of mind increases when we welcome God to participate in whatever we're involved in.

"God doesn't dispense strength and encouragement like a physician does medication. He doesn't give us something to 'take' to handle our anger. He gives us Himself. He says, 'Come to me, all you who are weary and burdened, and I will give you rest' (Matthew 11:28). God is our peace. He wants to give us rest. All He asks is that we come to Him, spend time with Him, talk to Him, and listen to His Spirit speak as we read the Scriptures. Might there be some ways you could invite God to be more involved in your life?"

Todd left his session with John that day challenged to think about how he could develop his relationship with God. He wanted God to become a higher priority. During a period of reevaluation, he decided to set aside the first half-hour of the day to read a devotional Bible and pray. He also decided that before going to bed at night, he would briefly review what he had read in the morning and remind himself of the thoughts that seemed particularly relevant to what was happening in his life. And last but not least, he decided to release the concerns of his day into God's care before he went to sleep.

As the months passed, Todd grew stronger in his relationship with God, and his emotional composure improved as well. In taking care of his physical, mental, and spiritual needs, Todd increased his ability to tolerate the frustrations that came in the course of a normal day. He still found himself frustrated and angry at times, as we all do, but he didn't get stuck in his anger. He had the inner stamina to work through his aggravations and let his anger go.

And then there is time in which to be, simply to be, that time in which God quietly tells us who we are and who he wants us to be. It is then that God can take our emptiness and fill it up with what he wants, and drain away the business with which we inevitably get involved in the dailiness of human living.

MADELEINE L'ENGLE

Chapter Nine

Rely on the Holy Spirit

My friends, be glad, even if you have a lot of trouble.

You know that you learn to endure

by having your faith tested.

If any of you need wisdom, you should ask God,

and it will be given to you.

JAMES 1:2–3, 5, CEV

WHEN WE FIND OURSELVES IN TENSE SITUATIONS, ONE WAY to reduce the aggressive, destructive element of our anger is to rely on the Holy Spirit. With His help, we can be passionately angry about something and still not blow it.

Every arena of life has its share of "difficult" people. We've all brushed shoulders with them: "tanks, snipers, exploders, complainers, bulldozers, wet blankets, silent clams, procrastinators, and know-it-alls."[1] And if we are honest, at one time or another we've probably adopted one or more of these roles ourselves and been someone else's difficult person.

When we come into conflict with difficult people, our natural human tendency is to strive for a position of apparent superiority. Instead of treating them with reason and respect, we seek to get the upper hand and press them under our thumb by sending cues that say "I'm better than you are." As Dr. Les Carter and Dr. Frank Minirth point out, this natural tendency to relate to others strictly on the basis of their performance only produces more anger:

> In any arena, be it job performance, emotional management, social skills, or Christian living, we feel compelled to grade the performance. Implied in any evaluation, no matter how positive, is the covertly communicated threat, "You'd better keep up the high performance or I'll be forced to tell you how bad you are." A strong emphasis on evaluation coupled with the inevitable inability for any of us to be perfect leads head-on to frustration and anger.[2]

When we act on our first impulse, we are prone to surrender to the unbridled desires of our darker side and act on shallow urges and fleeting passions rather than on our deeper values and convictions. If your son criticizes your viewpoint, instead of speaking to him with respect, you tell him he doesn't have a clue. If a coworker doesn't do things exactly the way you would, you make it your job to convey the message that he or she doesn't measure up. If your spouse can talk circles around you, you choose not to enter a discussion. This response to our anger, if allowed to dominate our interactions with others, will destroy our relationships and us.

People who are ruled by their desires
think only of themselves.
Everyone who is ruled by the Holy Spirit
thinks about spiritual things.
If our minds are ruled by our desires, we will die.
But if our minds are ruled by the Spirit,
we will have life and peace.

Romans 8:5–6, CEV

Ultimately, it boils down to this: When we're angry, we have to make a decision. Are we going to handle things ourselves, or are we going to ask God to guide us? All the Holy Spirit needs from us is an open mind and ten seconds—ten seconds when we tune in to Him and ask: *What do You want me to do? What do You want me to see? Show me. Lead me.* Successful anger management depends on our ability to rely on the Holy Spirit for whatever we need, whenever we need it. It comes as we yield to Him and let Him lead.

Successful anger management depends on our ability to rely on the Holy Spirit for whatever we need, whenever we need it.

God has a provision for every conflict we encounter. The bigger the problem, the bigger God's provision. When we ask the Holy Spirit to enlighten us, to give us His perspective, and to guide us and empower our responses, we are more likely to appropriately express our anger and use it for good. The question is: Are we going to tap into what God has to offer, or try to muscle through on our own?

Jesus made it clear that if we ask for God's provision, we will receive it:

> "Ask and it will be given to you; seek and you will find; knock and the door will be opened to you. For everyone who asks receives; he who seeks finds; and to him who knocks, the door will be opened. Which of you fathers, if your son asks for a fish, will give him a snake instead? Or if he asks for an egg, will give him a scorpion? If you then, though you are evil, know how to give good gifts to your children, how much more will your Father in heaven give the Holy Spirit to those who ask him!"
>
> LUKE 11:9–13

In the heat of a conflict, our natural human impulses can prompt us in directions that are completely opposite to where the Holy Spirit would lead us. He will never advise us to engage in one-upmanship, or prompt us to demean those who make mistakes or show signs of imperfection. He won't stir us up to manipulate circumstances to get even.

When we ask the Holy Spirit to rule our mind, will, and emotions, our responses to problematic issues will reflect His nature. He will guide us to value and treat others with a spirit of humility. He will lead us to speak in ways that are governed by reason, respect, and kindness. He will give us grace-filled eyes that focus on the tremendous intrinsic value and worth of each individual. He will press us to affirm others in their strengths and to assist them in their areas of weakness while speaking the truth in love. He will infuse our words and actions with love, joy, peace, patience, kindness, goodness, faithfulness, gentleness, and self-control (see Galatians 5:22–23). This is how good overcomes evil.

The bottom line is that we need God's help. We simply do not have God's ability to properly judge every situation accurately. We are limited in our understanding, in our courage, and in our ability to respond constructively to the harsh realities of life. That is why God gave us the Holy Spirit to be our companion, guide, and ongoing power supply. His resources are always sufficient and never ending.

I recall an occasion when the Holy Spirit gave John explicit instructions during an emotionally charged encounter with a difficult person, whom I'll call Cal. On several occasions when John and I were in Cal's company, I noticed some signs that Cal harbored ill feelings toward John. One time, John and I were in a room with a couple dozen other people. When one of the men in the group asked John to pray for him about something specific, I saw Cal surreptitiously roll his eyes and smirk. On another occasion I was casually chatting with Cal and a few others when John approached the group. Looking right past him, Cal abruptly left. I said nothing but asked God to bring to light whatever was necessary for harmony to prevail.

A few weeks later, someone confided to me that Cal had been talking about John in a negative fashion. When I heard this, I immediately became angry. *Why doesn't Cal talk to John directly if there's a problem?* I asked myself. I asked God what He wanted me to do with this troublesome information, and He said: *Nothing! Be quiet and pray.* So that's what I did. Again, I asked the Spirit of God to bring out into the open whatever needed to be revealed.

God answered that prayer. Shortly thereafter when John was in a meeting with Cal and several other people, Cal lashed out at him. With his voice raised and his eyes flaming, he castigated John for an error he had made while carrying out a certain task. When Cal continued to blast away, John asked, "Cal, why are you getting so angry?"

Cal's red-faced response was, "I'm not angry! You should have told us. . . ." Although John had admitted his error and committed himself to correcting the problem in the future, Cal's condescending comments continued.

John wanted to defend himself. It was humiliating to be attacked in front of his peers, and he felt like confronting Cal about his patronizing, "I'll show you who's better" attitude. But at that point, John sensed the Holy Spirit saying, *Be quiet. Don't defend yourself.* Cal's reaction was disproportionate to the infraction, and it occurred to John that something else might be fueling Cal's anger.

Love must be sincere.

Hate what is evil; cling to what is good.

Be devoted to one another in brotherly love.

Honor one another above yourselves.

Bless those who persecute you; bless and do not curse.

Romans 12:9–10, 14

When the meeting was over, John asked Cal if he would meet with him to talk further. Cal was noncommittal. John waited a few days and approached Cal a second time with a request that they meet over coffee. Cal put him off again, saying he would call John to schedule a time to meet. The call never came. A week later, John asked Cal a third time to get together, and finally Cal agreed.

When they met, John opened the discussion. "Cal, I know you're angry with me," he said, "and I want to understand why."

Much to John's surprise, Cal replied, "I've done a lot of thinking and praying about this, and I think I've been angry with you because I feel insecure and don't think you respect my position or support me."

"Is there anything that I've done that has made you think I'm not behind you?" John asked.

"No," Cal replied, shaking his head and looking at the floor. "I think this has more to do with me than it does with you."

John reassured Cal that he did respect him and his role. He affirmed his gifts and talents and told him that his contributions were invaluable. At the close of their time together they prayed for each other and embraced. The breach was repaired and unity was restored.

This never would have happened if both John and Cal hadn't been willing to follow through with what the Holy Spirit was leading them to do. John's instructions were to be quiet, to not defend himself, and to make an effort to understand. Cal's were to be emotionally honest and to admit his insecurities. When both men relied on the Spirit to lead, reconciliation occurred.

Sad to say, endings like this are not the norm. Far more relationships end in big blowouts over small issues because angry people don't rely on the Holy Spirit to guide them. Instead of inviting God to direct, they allow their emotions to rule. And when they do, the results can have a destructive impact on everyone involved.

One of the good things about struggling with anger is that it can help us see that we weren't built to live our lives apart from God. As we commune with the Holy Spirit and cultivate an intimate friendship with Him, He promises to give us whatever we need to respond to the challenges we face.

There is absolutely no frustration in your life that God doesn't know about. There is no difficulty that He can't help you handle, no aggravation that He can't use to teach you something about yourself. And there's no hardship that can't teach you something about God's goodness, faithfulness, and provision for your life. When you don't know the way, but you know the

Guide, you can have every confidence that He will order your steps and find a way through whatever problems are at hand. When you walk with God, you will get where He's going.

Following His lead, as He gives you the grace and power to do so, facilitates deep, long-lasting, positive change inside you—regardless of what is happening outside you. As you relax your grip and open-handedly offer your limited resources to God, He will do unlimited things. Good anger management isn't all up to you. It's a God-sized task, and rest assured, my friend, the Holy Spirit will give you what you need when you need it, so you can manage your anger effectively and eventually let it go.

The word "Comforter" as applied to the Holy Spirit
needs to be translated by some vigorous term.
Literally, it means "with strength."
Jesus promised his followers that
"The Strengthener" would be with them.
This promise is no lullaby for the fainthearted.
It is a blood transfusion for courageous living.

E. Paul Hovey

Chapter Ten

Renounce Replays and Revenge

He who seeks revenge digs two graves.

KEVIN, A FRIENDLY, MIDDLE-CLASS, LAW-ABIDING AMERICAN, works as a welder in town. A year ago, he had a good life. He enjoyed a warm relationship with his wife, worked a steady job from seven to three, and attended his children's Little League games on weekends. But one morning on his way to work, everything changed.

It was early, and Kevin's car was the only one on the road. As he approached a stop sign, he saw a pedestrian standing on the sidewalk. He thought the man was waiting to cross the street, so he rolled to a complete stop and motioned to him to go ahead. But the pedestrian shook his head and waved for him to pass. Kevin smiled, nodded, took a sip of his coffee, and pressed the accelerator. Just as he began moving forward, the man stepped toward the car, fell down, and started screaming, "You hit me! You hit me!" Kevin knew that the car hadn't touched the man, but he got out to check. When two other cars approached, the scam artist was hollering as if a truck going fifty miles an hour had hit him.

Today, Kevin is in the midst of a messy lawsuit. Although he knows that he's innocent, the memory of the incident haunts him. He hates the man for making his life a nightmare, and in an instinctive backlash against the one who is hurting him, he replays—over and over—the mental tape of that awful morning. Images of revenge energize him. He envisions finding the guy's house and setting it on fire. He fantasizes about hiring a hit man to take him out. He's suffering, and he wants his offender to suffer too.

These images of revenge are dangerous and can be deadly if allowed to run their course. Kevin can't eat. He can't sleep. He's like a ticking time bomb waiting to explode at the slightest hint that he will be the victim of another injustice. He's afraid of what he might do.

Most of us have found ourselves struggling with images of retribution after we've been wounded. "Treason!" we cry, and pictures of how we can get even flash before our eyes.

- A coworker tells me that I should be promoted to take on a certain task and then tells my superior that I'm not good enough to do the job. I imagine suggesting that he make hypocrisy the topic of his next Bible study.
- A trusted friend betrays your confidence and tells a person known to be a gossip something that you wanted to remain private. Now "everybody" knows. You see yourself backing your betrayer into a corner, giving her a vicious tongue-lashing, and then walking out on her for good.
- A wife sarcastically puts down her husband in front of dinner company. He envisions slapping her to set her straight.

- A father discovers that his thirty-year-old brother has been sexually assaulting his six-year-old daughter. He envisions his hands around his brother's throat.
- A husband watches reruns of two planes smashing into the World Trade Center where his wife was at work on September 11, 2001. He pictures himself bombing Muslim communities.

Replays don't divert anger; they sustain and fuel it. Our minds play reruns of those wretched events over and over and over again, and many of the replays are laced with fantasies of retribution. With each painful image, our dreams of retaliation grow crueler, and the chance that we will act on our anger increases. Every angry scene we relive pushes the adrenaline button in our body and throws us into 911 mode all over again. The more we rehearse our pain and fantasize revenge, the more we weaken our ability to control our impulses and set ourselves up to act in ways that can destroy us. Thoughts of being burned, cheated, and demeaned drive feelings of anger, humiliation, and hate...and they trap us in a torture chamber of our own making.

Replays don't divert anger; they sustain and fuel it.

But we don't have to live at the mercy of the violent images that keep us chained to our pain. We don't have to be victimized by runaway fantasies that poison our souls with bitterness and hate. There's a way to put an end to the hostile nightmares. There's an alternative to clinging to our lust for revenge.

It's called *forgiveness.*

Rehearsing our offender's evil deeds simply generates more evil in us. And one thing is certain: We cannot overcome evil with evil; we can only overcome evil with good. God is good, and He instructs us to forgive—not for His sake, but for ours. He knows that forgiveness is in our best interest and that it will work for our highest good.

Forgiveness and letting go of anger are one and the same. If we do not forgive, we sentence ourselves to a life imprisoned by pain. We freeze ourselves in the past, weigh ourselves down with heavy grudges, and become arrested in our grief. And we give our betrayers more power than they deserve by allowing them to repeatedly frustrate and immobilize us.

Does forgiveness come easily? I don't think so. Frankly, even the thought of forgiving a person who has wounded us can make us angry. We don't want to forgive because we don't want to let them off the hook. In a twisted sort of way, we're prone to think that our unforgiving spirit somehow holds our offenders accountable for their wrong and keeps them from wounding us again. We fear that if we forgive, we will be hurt again.

A husband whose wife had had an affair told John, "If I forgive her, she'll do it again." He was under the illusion that his lack of forgiveness was making her "toe the line" and keeping her in the marriage. But nothing could have been further from the truth. By hanging on to his anger, he was turning into a contemptuous crank and making it more likely that his wife would leave him. If we believe that there are benefits to not forgiving, we deceive ourselves.

When you release your grip on the wrong that was done to you by placing it in God's hands, you set yourself free from the prison of pain.

Forgiveness is not easy or natural. It is difficult and supernatural. It requires God's involvement. The more we've been hurt, the more we need God to enable us to forgive. Deeper wounds require greater grace. Forgiveness is a process, and in each step there are two parts: our part and God's part. As we do ours, He does His. Walking through these steps with the Holy Spirit will give you the help you need to forgive those who have hurt you.

F: Face the Facts

Our Part

We face our explosive sense of injustice and admit that we have been rehearsing the wrongs done to us. We acknowledge that these obsessions have fueled our anger and hate. We admit our powerlessness to let go of our anger, and we ask God to forgive us for the ill will we have wished others.

God's Part

God forgives us. His Word assures us that this is so. "A broken and contrite heart, O God, you will not despise" (Psalm 51:17). "If we admit our sins—make a clean breast of them—he won't let us down; he'll be true to himself. He'll forgive our sins and purge us of all wrongdoing" (1 John 1:9, *The Message*).

O: Obstruct Thoughts of Revenge

Our Part

When memories of our pain are triggered—as they will be—and we are tempted to envision revenge, we take control and immediately stop this mental process. We capture our thoughts and make them work for us instead of against us. One way to divert these violent thoughts is to boldly say, "Stop! It's not my job to balance the scales; it's God's job. Let it go!" We believe God when He says "It is mine to avenge; I will repay" (Hebrews 10:30).

God's Part

God keeps His promises; He will do what He says He will do. He will hold all of us, including those who have wounded us, accountable. "Each of us will give an account of himself to God" (Romans 14:12).

R: Relinquish Your Will

Our Part

Next, we ask God to do what we cannot do. We pray, *God, I cannot forgive, but I am willing to be willing. Give me Your heart and mind in this situation. Help me perceive the one who hurt me from Your perspective. Do a creative work in my heart that will enable me to let go of my anger. Lead me to the place of understanding and empathy Jesus experienced when He prayed on behalf of His murderers: "Father, forgive them, for they know not what they do"* (Luke 23:34, KJV).

God's Part

In response to our cries for help, God promises to change us. He softens our stubborn, defensive hearts by the power of His Spirit within us. He says: "*I will* give them an undivided heart and put a new spirit in them; *I will* remove from them their heart of stone and give them a heart of flesh" (Ezekiel 11:19, emphasis added).

G: Grant Them Forgiveness

Our Part

We do what the apostle Paul tells us to do: "Be…quick to forgive an offense. Forgive as quickly and completely as the Master forgave you" (Colossians 3:13, *The Message*). We make a deliberate choice to forgive those who have hurt us, and we name the date and time we do it. This has nothing to do with feelings or emotions. It is a tough-minded decision of the will.

God's Part

Over time, God heals our emotions. God "heals the brokenhearted and binds up their wounds" (Psalm 147:3). He restores, renews, and refreshes us until our feelings catch up with our mental assent to let the anger go.

I: Inspect Yourself

Our Part

We shift our focus away from those who have hurt us and concentrate on being who God wants *us* to be.

> "Do not judge, or you too will be judged. For in the same way you judge others, you will be judged, and with the measure you use, it will be measured to you. Why do you look at the speck of sawdust in your brother's eye and pay no attention to the plank in your own eye? How can you say to your brother, 'Let me take the speck out of your eye,' when all the time there is a plank in your own eye? You hypocrite, first take the plank out of your own eye, and then you will see clearly to remove the speck from your brother's eye."
>
> Matthew 7:1–5

God's Part

As we keep our focus on being who God wants us to be, the qualities of His character increase in us, and our negative traits decrease. He gives us new perspectives laced with humility, understanding, and empathy, and these insights lead to new feelings. "Love comes from God" (1 John 4:7, *The Message*), and His love gradually eclipses our anger.

V: Validate Their Worth

Our Part

We pray for those who have hurt us. "Pray for those who persecute you" (Matthew 5:44). If we don't know where to start, we ask God or someone we trust to guide us.

God's Part

God teaches us how to pray for those who have hurt us. He gives us the words to say. He gives us the power to release others from our judgment whenever our pain resurfaces.

E: Exercise Compassion

Our Part

We bless those who hurt us. "No retaliation. No sharp-tongued sarcasm. Instead, bless—that's your job, to bless. You'll be a blessing and also get a blessing" (1 Peter 3:9, *The Message*).

God's Part

God blesses us with His goodness and favor in ways we never imagined or expected. "Whoever wants to embrace life and see the day fill up with good, here's what you do: say nothing evil or hurtful; snub evil and cultivate good; run after peace for all you're worth. God looks on all this with approval, listening and responding well to what he's asked" (1 Peter 3:10–12, *The Message*).

Even with the help of the Holy Spirit, it takes time to get through these steps. Forgiveness is not an instantaneous event. Progress in healing occurs in inches, not miles. It's typically a very slow process that rarely happens as smoothly or as quickly as we'd like. But the day will come when we're able to bless those who curse us, and when it does, we can know that we have a forgiving spirit. Our friend Graham comes to mind.

Graham is a gifted teacher and educator who travels internationally speaking on a variety of subjects. Years ago, reports began filtering back to him that a prominent preacher of an independent church in town was publicly ridiculing him.

The verbal assaults continued week after week, and people in the community made it their business to tell him what was being said.

Months later, news came that this bad-mouthing preacher was losing people from his congregation and that the church was struggling to survive. Graham's loyal friends said to him, "Hey, that guy's getting what he deserves! God is taking revenge on him for the way he's been attacking you. Aren't you glad?"

But Graham wasn't glad. He was grieved because he knew that other innocent people were being hurt as things fell apart. It didn't make him happy to see relationships ruined and people left out in the cold.

God, what do You want me to do? Graham prayed. *How do You want me to respond to this one who is cursing me?*

An idea came to mind: *Pay his salary.*

But, God! Graham argued. *He would never take a penny from me! He hates everything about me.*

Another thought came: *Then do it in a way that he won't know it's from you.*

Graham followed that prompting. For many months, he traveled across town in the middle of the night and dropped an envelope of cash through the mail slot of the preacher's front door. Before he left, he asked God to bless the man, his home, and his family. No one knew and no one found out. The blessing was between Graham and God.

Reports of the accusations against Graham gradually ceased, and one day he crossed paths with his adversary at a city-wide meeting for ministers. When Graham asked him how things were going for him, the man admitted that he was struggling.

"Is there any way I can help you?" Graham asked.

Visibly shaken, the man hung his head. Then, breaking the awkward silence, he said, "I need to apologize to you. I have a big mouth." Graham put his arms around the man and embraced him while he wept. Since that day the two have been friends.

When others hurt you in ways you don't deserve, at some point you will come to the crossroad of decision. You'll have to look your pain square in the face and ask, *Am I going to hang on to my anger and do violence to myself, or am I going to forgive those who have wounded me and let the anger go?*

Are you ready to stop doing violence to yourself? If so, commit yourself to taking the steps that will enable you to forgive. You might find this symbolic exercise useful in sealing your commitment:

Think about one person who has hurt you. Imagine yourself taking the angry images and vengeful thoughts you've had toward that person and putting them in both of your hands. Now close your hands and clench them tight. Focus on those clenched fists. Notice the pain and throbbing in your hands. All those ugly obsessions and resulting emotions are there in your tight grip.

Now lift your fists as high as you can toward heaven and open your hands before God. Give Him everything: Your anger. Your hate. Your bitterness. Your lust for revenge. Then offer Him your life: Your mind. Your will. Your emotions. Your agenda. Your past. Your present. Your future. All of it. Give it all up to Him. Let it go.

Do this again and again, seventy times seven, if the need arises.

Peter asked, "Lord, how often shall my brother sin against me and I forgive him? Up to seven times?" Jesus said to him, "I do not say to you, up to seven times, but up to seventy times seven" (Matthew 18:21–22, NASB). What this verse says to me is that we will find ourselves in difficult situations where we will have to forgive again and again and again. Forgiveness is a discipline we must practice on a regular basis. But as we do our part, God will always do His. When we relax our grip and open our hands to Him, we will give Him a new place to deposit whatever we need to let our anger go.

[Jesus said,] "Are you tired? Worn out?
Burned out on religion?
Come to me. Get away with me and
you'll recover your life.
I'll show you how to take a real rest.
Walk with me and work with me—watch how I do it.
Learn the unforced rhythms of grace.
I won't lay anything heavy or ill-fitting on you.
Keep company with me and you'll learn to
live freely and lightly."

MATTHEW 11:28–30, *THE MESSAGE*

Multnomah Publishers
The publisher and author would love to hear your comments about this book. *Please contact us at:*
www.multnomah.net/lettinggo

Group Discussion Questions

Chapter 1. Remember: It's Okay to Be Angry

1. Anger is part of God's original design, a legitimate response to certain situations. What are some of the positive functions of anger?
2. Read the three passages in Mark again (Mark 3:5; 10:13–16; 11:15–17). What kinds of things fueled Christ's anger?
3. What are your hopes and fears as you begin this study on frustration and anger? With the rest of your group, commit these hopes to God in prayer.

Chapter 2: Recognize Your Anger Style

1. What are some biological and psychological reasons for anger?
2. As children, we usually learn to deal with anger by observing those around us. How did your mother express her anger? Your father? Your siblings? How do you typically express your anger?

3. What would you like to change about the way you handle frustrating and stressful events? Decide on a goal and share it with the group. As a group, pray for one another and the attainment of these goals.

CHAPTER 3: RECITE THE ABCs OF ANGER

1. When you read the statement "I make me mad," what thoughts went through your mind?
2. *A* stands for activating event, *B* stands for beliefs, and *C* stands for consequences. Using the space below, record a scenario from this past week when you felt angry. Then discuss your chart with the rest of your group.

Activating Event	Beliefs	Consequences

3. *Shoulds*, *oughts*, *musts*, and *have to*s fuel anger, in ourselves and in others. What kinds of *shoulds* typically fill your thoughts? Discuss them with the group, and pray with one another for God's help in erasing them from your mental vocabulary.

CHAPTER 4: REMAIN CALM

1. What is the PPP strategy? Tell the group about one specific situation last week when it would have been helpful to have used it.
2. Using cool words, write five calming statements that you can use this week to stop the escalation of anger when you find yourself frustrated and angry.

3. Pray for each person in the group. Talk to God about the burdens of your heart that fuel your anger.

Chapter 5: Relinquish Control

1. Can you recall times when you have become angry in response to another person's control tactics? Can you recall times when you have tried to control others and they have responded with anger?
2. What insights did you glean from this chapter? Can you identify a situation where you may need to be less controlling and step back and let go? What might letting go look like? What specific steps could you take to put it into practice this week?
3. When we let go, we stop trying to do the impossible and focus on what is possible. Why do you think it is so difficult to relinquish control? Pray for one another to grow in the ability to surrender to God.

Chapter 6: Resolve Unmet Needs

1. How are anger and unmet needs related?
2. We all have perceived needs: for rest, time alone, time with friends, recreation, good meals, exercise, mental and spiritual growth, and so on. Identify one of your needs that you think is not adequately met, and brainstorm with your group some ways that you could meet it.
3. Evaluate your expectations. Can you pinpoint one unrealistic expectation that may be fueling unnecessary distress? Ask your group for help in revising that expectation. Pray for one another, asking for God's assistance in meeting your unmet needs.

Chapter 7: Resist the Pharisee Syndrome

1. When we play the role of Pharisee, we set ourselves up for anger and grieve the Holy Spirit. As you read my story, did a similar situation in your life come to mind? When is it easy for you to slip into the Pharisee role? What are the results?
2. The realization that "this is not what I want" triggers anger and presents us with a choice. We can act like petulant children and argue, resist, slam doors, withdraw, and pout, or we can surrender to God and trust that He has a good plan for our lives and that He is working it out on schedule. Where are you in this process as you think about the hard realities in your life?
3. Reread Jeremiah 18:1–6. How might these verses apply to what you are going through right now?

Chapter 8: Rest and Renew

1. Do you tend to burn the candle at both ends and persistently push yourself? What are the payoffs of doing this? What are the costs?
2. What is one step you could take this week to renew your body, mind, and spirit?
3. If we find ourselves perpetually irritable and angry, something in our life needs attention. We need to heed these red flags and give ourselves grace. Pray together, asking God to show you some concrete ways that you can improve your self-care. Ask Him to empower each group member to follow through with these ideas this week.

Chapter 9: Rely on the Holy Spirit

1. What do we mean when we say that "all the Holy Spirit needs from us is an open mind and ten seconds"?
2. Can you think of a time when you were angry and you responded by following God's lead instead of your own natural impulses? Describe the scenario to the group. What were the results?
3. Set a goal to abide by the "ten-second tune-in" rule this week. Commit this goal to God in prayer, asking for the Holy Spirit to fine-tune your spiritual ears so that you can follow His lead. When you get together with your group again, tell them what happened when you asked for God's wisdom and then acted on it.

Chapter 10: Renounce Replays and Revenge

1. Replays don't divert anger; they sustain and fuel it. Have you found this to be true in your life? What makes it difficult for you to stop the replays?
2. Forgiveness is not an easy or quick process. What has helped you to be able to forgive someone who hurt you?
3. The process of forgiveness has two parts: your part and God's part. Think about a specific person with whom you are angry. What is your part? What is God's part? As a group, pray together, asking for God's supernatural assistance in letting go of your anger.

Notes

Chapter Two

1. Dr. Theo Johnson, *Velvet Steel Anger Control Manual* (Gresham, Ore.: Healing Touch Ministries, 2000), 8. For more information, contact Dr. Johnson at www.healing-touchministries.org.
2. Dr. Willard Gaylan, *The Rage Within: Anger in Modern Life* (New York: Penguin Publishers, 1989), n.p.

Chapter Three

1. Dr. Albert Ellis, *Reason and Emotion in Psychotherapy* (New York: Carol Publishing Group, 1994), n.p.

Chapter Six

1. Dr. Ted Roberts, *Pure Desire* (Ventura, Calif.: Regal Books, 1999), 52.
2. Henri Nouwen, *The Road to Daybreak: A Spiritual Journey* (New York: Doubleday, 1988), 64–6.

Chapter Seven

1. Adapted from Pam Vredevelt, *Espresso for a Woman's Spirit, Book* 2 (Sisters, Ore.: Multnomah Publishers, 2001), 116–21.
2. Adapted from Pam Vredevelt, *Espresso for a Woman's Spirit* (Sisters, Ore.: Multnomah Publishers, 2000), 124–8.

Chapter Nine

1. Robert Bramson discusses these different types in *Coping With Difficult People* (New York: Ballantine, 1981).
2. Dr. Les Carter and Dr. Frank Minirth, *The Anger Workbook* (Nashville, Tenn.: Thomas Nelson Publishers, 1993), 182.

LET GO AND LET GOD

Attention, chronic worriers: It is possible to reduce the intensity, frequency, and duration of painful episodes of anxiety without medication. Licensed counselor Pam Vredevelt draws from twenty years of clinical experience, scientific research, and scriptural insight to offer the reader tools for living a more peaceful and tranquil life. While worrying is for many a deeply embedded habit, because it was learned, it can be "unlearned." With compassion and sound advice, Pam shows how.

ISBN 1-57673-955-4

Professional counselor Pam Vredevelt constantly hears the question, "How do I let go of the pain I feel?" Whether it is a soured friendship or a dissatisfying job, a wayward child or unrealistic expectations, every person has to deal with lingering disappointment and its clouding effect on attitude and relationships. God does not intend that pain to cripple, distort, and consume his children. Getting "unstuck" is possible, Pam writes, through the use of a few simple and practical tools that lead to peace of mind and tranquility of heart. We've all heard the expression, "Let go and let God." With compassion and warmth, Pam Vredevelt shows how.

ISBN 1-57673-954-6

Espresso for Your Spirit

In engaging, humorous, and often poignant vignettes, bestselling author Pam Vredevelt serves up cup after cup of energizing espresso to encourage the spirits of overwhelmed and exhausted parents.

ISBN 1-57673-485-4

Espresso for a Woman's Spirit

Exhaustion doesn't have to be habit-forming! Overcome it with humorous and poignant vignettes that bring refreshment to the soul the way espresso brings energy to the body.

ISBN 1-57673-636-9

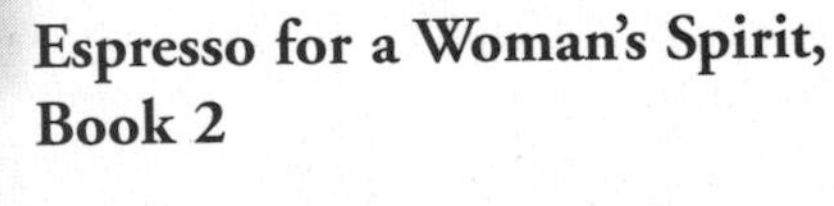

Espresso for a Woman's Spirit, Book 2

Espresso for a Woman's Spirit, Book 2 will reenergize the lagging spirit! Pam Vredevelt's funny and poignant real-life stories remind readers that God is always faithful, always at work, and always full of everything we lack, including guidance, love, compassion, and strength.

ISBN 1-57673-986-4

Hope and Support for Those Who Have Suffered a Miscarriage, Stillbirth, or Tubal Pregnancy

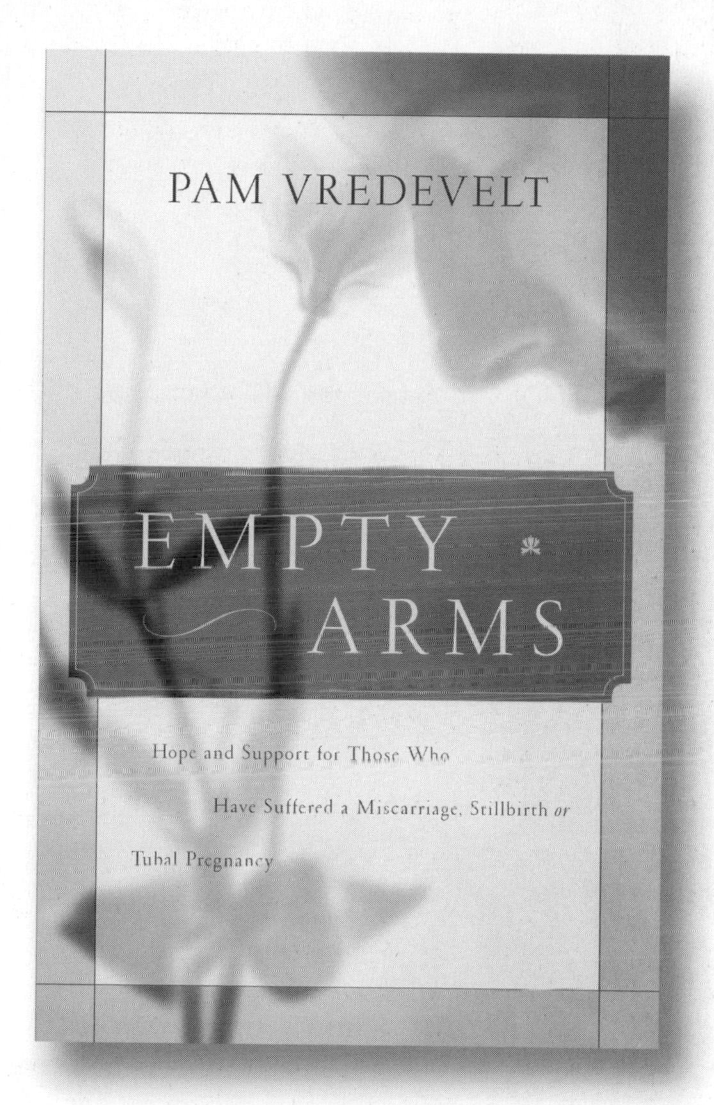

Having lost a child, the author writes with compassionate insight to women and their families, addressing grief, anger, guilt, spiritual battles, and other pertinent topics.

ISBN 1-57673-851-5

In Your Darkest Place, You May Find a Glimpse of Glory

Brimming with moving personal stories, *Angel Behind the Rocking Chair* offers hope and encouragement to those facing unexpected adversity. Each story is a reassuring reminder of God's unfailing love.

ISBN 1-57673-644-X